Preface

Have you already taken a CDMP (Certified Data Man
Fundamentals course from a Registered Training Prov

Or

Have you self-studied using the DAMA - DMBOK2?

Are you still not quite confident that you are ready to take the certification exam? *If so, you've come to the right place!*

Guideline to get most out of this book:

1. Study the applicable chapter in the DMBOK2.
2. Summarize the most important points in the chapter.
3. Take the quiz for the applicable chapters and check your answers.
4. If there are incorrect answers, refer back to the DMBOK2 and your notes.
5. Retake the quiz on a chapter and try to achieve a higher score (>80%).
6. Finally, when you are ready, take the practice exams at the end. You will have 90 minutes in the actual examination to complete the 100 questions.

Please take note of the question type when completing the questions:

Multiple-choice: One correct answer

Multi-select: One or multiple correct answers

Disclaimer

The questions in this book have been formulated on the chapters in DMBOK2. The DMBOK2 should first be procured and studied before attempting these questions. It is also recommended to attend an official course from a Registered Training Provider. These questions are not official training material for the CDMP and not endorsed by DAMA. They were purely constructed to provide final revision and solidify knowledge.

Contents

Correct Response

At the top of each page the correct response to the question on the previous page will be stated.

Explanation

The page in DMBOK2 will be referenced for your convenience.

Knowledge Area

The chapter name.

Chapter 1

Question 1

Please select the correct definition of Data Management from the options below.

Question Type

multiple-choice

Answer 1

Data Management is the strict control of all plans, policies, programs and practices that enable the business strategy to be successfully executed.

Answer 2

Data Management is the development, execution and supervision of plans, policies, programs and practices that deliver, control, protect and enhance the value of data and information assets throughout their lifecycles.

Answer 3

Data Management is the development, execution and supervision of plans, policies, programs and practices that deliver, control, protect and enhance the value of data assets throughout their lifecycles.

Answer 4

Data Management is the development, execution and supervision of plans, policies, programs and practices that deliver, control, protect and enhance the value of information assets throughout their lifecycles.

Correct Response

2

Explanation

Please refer to page 17 of DMBOK2.

Knowledge Area

Data Management

Question 2

Data Management Professionals only work with the technical aspects related to data.

Question Type

multiple-choice

Answer 1

True

Answer 2

False

Question 3

Differentiating between data and information. Please select the correct answers based on the sentence below:

Here is a marketing report for the last month [1]. It is based on data from our data warehouse [2]. Next month these results [3] will be used to generate our month-over-month performance measure [4].

Question Type

multiple-choice

Answer 1

[1] Information, [2] Information, [3] Data, [4] Information

Answer 2

[1] Data, [2] Information, [3] Data, [4] Data

Answer 3

[1] Data, [2] Data, [3] Data, [4] Information

Answer 4

[1] Information, [2] Data, [3] Data, [4] Information

Correct Response

4

Explanation

Please refer to page 17 of DMBOK2.

Knowledge Area

Data Management

Question 4

Please select the answers that correctly describes the set of principles that recognizes salient features of data management and guide data management practice.

Question Type

multi-select

Answer 1

Data is an asset with unique properties.

Answer 2

It takes Metadata to manage data.

Answer 3

The most important part of data management is security.

Answer 4

Data management is lifecycle management.

Answer 5

Effective data management requires leadership commitment.

Answer 6

Efficient data management requires a team of IT professionals only.

Correct Response

1,2,4,5

Explanation

Please refer to page 22-23 of DMBOK2.

Knowledge Area

Data Management

Question 5

Value is the difference between the cost of a thing and the benefit derived from that thing.

Question Type

multiple-choice

Answer 1

True

Answer 2

False

Correct Response

1

Explanation

Please refer to page 24 of DMBOK2.

Knowledge Area

Data Management

Question 6

Please select the correct general cost and benefit categories that can be applied consistently within an organization.

Question Type

multi-select

Answer 1

Cost of erasing data from servers

Answer 2

Cost of improving data

Answer 3

What the data could be sold for

Answer 4

Benefit of higher quality data

Answer 5

Cost of replacing data if it were lost

Answer 6

What competitors would pay for data

Question 7

Please select the answers that correctly describes where the costs of poor quality data comes from.

Question Type

multi-select

Answer 1

Scrap and rework

Answer 2

Organizational conflict

Answer 3

High job satisfaction

Answer 4

High productivity

Answer 5

Reputational costs

Answer 6

Compliance costs

Correct Response

1,2,5,6

Explanation

Please refer to page 25-26 of DMBOK2.

Knowledge Area

Data Management

Question 8

Reduced risk is a benefit of high quality data.

Question Type

multiple-choice

Answer 1

True

Answer 2

False

Correct Response

1

Explanation

Please refer to page 25-26 of DMBOK2.

Knowledge Area

Data Management

Question 9

The better an organization understands the lifecycle and lineage of its data, the better able it will be to manage its data. Please select correct implication of the focus of data management on the data lifecycle.

Question Type

multiple-choice

Answer 1

Data Quality must be managed throughout the data lifecycle

Answer 2

Data Security must only be managed at the start of the data lifecycle

Answer 3

Metadata Quality is the most important part of the management process

Answer 4

Data Management efforts should focus on the most critical data last

Question 10

Information gaps represent enterprise liabilities with potentially profound impacts on operational effectiveness and profitability.

Question Type

multiple-choice

Answer 1

True

Answer 2

False

Correct Response

1

Explanation

Please refer to page 30 of DMBOK2.

Knowledge Area

Data Management

Chapter 2

Question 1

Data handling ethics are concerned with how to procure, store, manage, use and dispose of data in ways that are aligned with ethical principles.

Question Type

multiple-choice

Answer 1

True

Answer 2

False

Correct Response

1

Explanation

Please refer to page 49 of DMBOK2.

Knowledge Area

Data Handling Ethics

Question 2

The ethics of data handling are complex, but is centred on several core concepts. Please select the correct answers.

Question Type

multi-select

Answer 1

Impact on machines

Answer 2

Impact on people

Answer 3

Potential for data management

Answer 4

Potential for misuse

Answer 5

Economic value of ethics

Answer 6

Economics value of data

Correct Response

2,4,6

Explanation

Please refer to page 49 of DMBOK2.

Knowledge Area

Data Handling Ethics

Question 3

Within the Data Handling Ethics Context Diagram a key deliverable is the Ethical Data Handling Strategy.

Question Type

multiple-choice

Answer 1

True

Answer 2

False

Correct Response

1

Explanation

Please refer to page 50 of DMBOK2.

Knowledge Area

Data Handling Ethics

Question 4

The Belmont principles that may be adapted for Information Management disciplines, include:

Question Type

multi-select

Answer 1

Respect for Persons

Answer 2

Respect for Machines

Answer 3

Beneficence

Answer 4

Criminality

Answer 5

Justice

Correct Response

1,3,5

Explanation

Please refer to page 52 of DMBOK2.

Knowledge Area

Data Handling Ethics

Question 5

Please select the correct principles of the General Data Protection Regulation (GDPR) of the EU.

Question Type

multi-select

Answer 1

Purpose Limitation

Answer 2

Data Minimisation

Answer 3

Accuracy

Answer 4

Storage Limitation

Answer 5

Accountability

Answer 6

All of the above

Question 6

Misleading visualisations could be an example where a base level of truthfulness and transparency are not adhered to.

Question Type

multiple-choice

Answer 1

True

Answer 2

False

Correct Response

1

Explanation

Please refer to page 57 of DMBOK2.

Knowledge Area

Data Handling Ethics

Question 7

Bias refers to an inclination of outlook. Please select the types of data bias:

Question Type

multi-select

Answer 1

Data collection for pre-defined results

Answer 2

Hunch and search

Answer 3

Positive reinforcement

Answer 4

Context and Emotion

Answer 5

Biased use of data collected

Answer 6

Biased sampling methodology

Question 8

If data is not integrated with care it presents risk for unethical data handling. These ethical risks intersect with fundamental problems in data management including: Limited knowledge of data's origin and lineage; Data of poor quality; Unreliable Metadata; and Documentation of error remediation.

Question Type

multiple-choice

Answer 1

True

Answer 2

False

Correct Response

2

Explanation

Please refer to page 59-60 of DMBOK2.

Knowledge Area

Data Handling Ethics

Question 9

Obfuscating or redacting data is the practice of making information anonymous ot removing sensitive information. Risks are present in the following instances:

Question Type

multi-select

Answer 1

Data storage

Answer 2

Data marketing

Answer 3

Data aggregation

Answer 4

Data marking

Answer 5

Data masking

Answer 6

Data integration

Question 10

Improving an organization's ethical behaviour requires an informal Organizational Change Management (OCM) process.

Question Type

multiple-choice

Answer 1

True

Answer 2

False

Correct Response

2

Explanation

Please refer to page 61 of DMBOK2.

Knowledge Area

Data Handling Ethics

Chapter 3

Question 1

The purpose of data governance is to ensure that data is managed properly, according to policies and best practices. Data governance is focused on how decisions are made about data and how people and processes are expected to behave in relation to data.

Question Type

multiple-choice

Answer 1

True

Answer 2

False

Correct Response

1

Explanation

Please refer to page 67-68 of DMBOK2.

Knowledge Area

Data Governance

Question 2

The scope and focus of any data governance program depend on organizational needs, but most programs include:

Question Type

multi-select

Answer 1

Strategy

Answer 2

Policy

Answer 3

Data Management Projects

Answer 4

Compliance

Answer 5

Oversight

Answer 6

All of the above

Correct Response

6

Explanation

Please refer to page 68 of DMBOK2.

Knowledge Area

Data Governance

Question 3

A goal of data governance is to enable an organisation to manage its data as a liability.

Question Type

multiple-choice

Answer 1

True

Answer 2

False

Correct Response

2

Explanation

Please refer to page 69 of DMBOK2.

Knowledge Area

Data Governance

Question 4

Drivers for data governance most often focus on reducing risk or improving processes. Please select the elements that relate to the reduction in risk:

Question Type

multi-select

Answer 1

Specific risk management

Answer 2

General risk management

Answer 3

Data ethics

Answer 4

Data security

Answer 5

Publicity

Answer 6

Privacy

Question 5

Drivers for data governance most often focus on reducing risk or improving processes. Please select the elements that relate to the improvement of processes:

Question Type

multi-select

Answer 1

Regulatory compliance

Answer 2

Data quality improvements

Answer 3

Metadata management

Answer 4

Efficiency in development projects

Answer 5

Vendor management

Answer 6

All of the above

Correct Response

6

Explanation

Please refer to page 70 of DMBOK2.

Knowledge Area

Data Governance

Question 6

Data governance and IT governance are the same thing.

Question Type

multiple-choice

Answer 1

True

Answer 2

False

Correct Response

2

Explanation

Please refer to page 71 of DMBOK2.

Knowledge Area

Data Governance

Question 7

Select three correct attributes a data governance programme must be:

Question Type

multi-select

Answer 1

Embedded

Answer 2

Flexible

Answer 3

Measures

Answer 4

Rigid

Answer 5

Independent responsibility

Answer 6

Sustainable

Correct Response

1,3,6

Explanation

Please refer to page 71 of DMBOK2.

Knowledge Area

Data Governance

Question 8

Governance ensures data is managed, but is not include the actual act of managing data.

Question Type

multiple-choice

Answer 1

True

Answer 2

False

Question 9

Data governance can be understood in terms of political governance. It includes the following three function types:

Question Type

multi-select

Answer 1

Legislative-like functions

Answer 2

Judicial-like functions

Answer 3

Ethical-like functions

Answer 4

Executive functions

Answer 5

Data-like functions

Answer 6

Morality-like functions

Correct Response

1,2,4

Explanation

Please refer to page 73-74 of DMBOK2.

Knowledge Area

Data Governance

Question 10

The Data Governance Council (DGC) manages data governance initiatives, issues, and escalations.

Question Type

multiple-choice

Answer 1

True

Answer 2

False

Correct Response

1

Explanation

Please refer to page 74 of DMBOK2.

Knowledge Area

Data Governance

Question 11

Data Governance Office (DGO) focuses on enterprise-level data definitions and data management standards across all DAMA-DMBOK knowledge areas. Consists of coordinating data management roles.

Question Type

multiple-choice

Answer 1

True

Answer 2

False

Correct Response

1

Explanation

Please refer to page 74 of DMBOK2.

Knowledge Area

Data Governance

Question 12

Three data governance operating models types include:

Question Type

multi-select

Answer 1

Centralized

Answer 2

Decentralized

Answer 3

Feathered

Answer 4

Federated

Answer 5

Replicated

Answer 6

Duplicated

Correct Response

1,4,5

Explanation

Please refer to page 75 of DMBOK2.

Knowledge Area

Data Governance

Question 13

Data stewardship is the least common label to describe accountability and responsibility for data and processes to ensure effective control and use of data assets.

Question Type

multiple-choice

Answer 1

True

Answer 2

False

Question 14

Please select the correct types of data stewards:

Question Type

multi-select

Answer 1

Executive Data Steward

Answer 2

Chief Data Steward

Answer 3

Enterprise Data Steward

Answer 4

Business Data Steward

Answer 5

A Data Seller

Answer 6

All of the above

Correct Response

1,2,3,4

Explanation

Please refer to page 76-77 of DMBOK2.

Knowledge Area

Data Governance

Question 15

Data asset valuation is the process of understanding and calculating the economic value of data to an organisation. Value comes when the economic benefit of using data outweighs the costs of acquiring and storing it, as

Question Type

multiple-choice

Answer 1

True

Answer 2

False

Correct Response

1

Explanation

Please refer to page 77 of DMBOK2.

Knowledge Area

Data Governance

Question 16

Some ways to measure value of data include:

Question Type

multi-select

Answer 1

Replacement cost

Answer 2

Market value

Answer 3

Selling Data

Answer 4

Risk cost

Answer 5

Identified opportunities

Answer 6

All of the above

Explanation

Please refer to page 78 of DMBOK2.

Knowledge Area

Data Governance

Question 17

Please select the correct General Accepted Information Principles:

Question Type

multi-select

Answer 1

Asset Principle

Answer 2

Audit Principle

Answer 3

Due Diligence Principle

Answer 4

Going Concern Principle

Answer 5

Ethical Principle

Answer 6

All of the above

Correct Response

1,2,3,4

Explanation

Please refer to page 78 of DMBOK2.

Knowledge Area

Data Governance

Question 18

Data governance program must contribute to the organization by identifying and delivering on specific benefits.

Question Type

multiple-choice

Answer 1

True

Answer 2

False

Correct Response

1

Explanation

Please refer to page 80 of DMBOK2.

Knowledge Area

Data Governance

Question 19

Part of alignment includes developing organizational touchpoints for data governance work. Some examples of touchpoints include: Procurement and Contracts; Budget and Funding; Regulatory Compliance; and the SDLC framework.

Question Type

multiple-choice

Answer 1

True

Answer 2

False

Explanation

Please refer to page 81 of DMBOK2.

Knowledge Area

Data Governance

Question 20

A data governance strategy defines the scope and approach to governance efforts. Deliverables include:

Question Type

multi-select

Answer 1

Charter

Answer 2

Operating framework and accountabilities

Answer 3

Implementation roadmap

Answer 4

Plan for operational success

Answer 5

All of the above

Answer 6

None of the above

Correct Response

5

Explanation

Please refer to page 82 of DMBOK2.

Knowledge Area

Data Governance

Chapter 4

Question 1

Architecture is the fundamental organization of a system, embodied in its components, their relationships to each other and the environment and the principles governing its design and evolution.

Question Type

multiple-choice

Answer 1

True

Answer 2

False

Correct Response

1

Explanation

Please refer to page 97-98 of DMBOK2.

Knowledge Area

Data Architecture

Question 2

Enterprise Architecture domains include:

Question Type

multi-select

Answer 1

Business Architecture

Answer 2

Data Architecture

Answer 3

Data Management Architecture

Answer 4

Systems Architecture

Answer 5

Application Architecture

Answer 6

Technology Architecture

Correct Response

1,2,5,6

Explanation

Please refer to page 98 of DMBOK2.

Knowledge Area

Data Architecture

Question 3

The most informal enterprise data model is the most detailed data architecture design document.

Question Type

multiple-choice

Answer 1

True

Answer 2

False

Explanation

Please refer to page 98 of DMBOK2.

Knowledge Area

Data Architecture

Question 4

The goal of data architecture is to:

Question Type

multiple-choice

Answer 1

Serve as a platform to enable data governance and management

Answer 2

Bridge between business strategy and technology execution

Answer 3

Provide the organisation with clear system of the architecture

Answer 4

Make the integration between data management and data analytics possible

Correct Response

2

Explanation

Please refer to page 99 of DMBOK2.

Knowledge Area

Data Architecture

Question 5

Data architects facilitate alignment between [1] and [2]

Question Type

multiple-choice

Answer 1

[1] Business and [2] IT

Answer 2

[1] Technology and [2] Data

Answer 3

[1] Governance and [2] Management

Answer 4

[1] Strategy and [2] Execution

Correct Response

1

Explanation

Please refer to page 99 of DMBOK2.

Knowledge Area

Data Architecture

Question 6

A goal of data architecture is to identify data storage and processing requirements.

Question Type

multiple-choice

Answer 1

True

Answer 2

False

Question 7

The deliverables in the data architecture context diagram include:

Question Type

multi-select

Answer 1

Data flows

Answer 2

Enterprise data

Answer 3

Implementation roadmap

Answer 4

Data Value Chains

Answer 5

None of the above

Answer 6

All of the above

Correct Response

6

Explanation

Please refer to page 100 of DMBOK2.

Knowledge Area

Data Architecture

Question 8

The purpose of enterprise application architecture is to describe the structure and functionality of applications in an enterprise.

Question Type

multiple-choice

Answer 1

True

Answer 2

False

Correct Response

1

Explanation

Please refer to page 101 of DMBOK2.

Knowledge Area

Data Architecture

Question 9

The dependencies of enterprise technology architecture are that it acts on specified data according to business requirements.

Question Type

multiple-choice

Answer 1

True

Answer 2

False

Correct Response

2

Explanation

Please refer to page 102 of DMBOK2.

Knowledge Area

Data Architecture

Question 10

The roles associated with enterprise data architecture are data architect, data modellers and data stewards.

Question Type

multiple-choice

Answer 1

True

Answer 2

False

Correct Response

1

Explanation

Please refer to page 102 of DMBOK2.

Knowledge Area

Data Architecture

Question 11

The Zachman Framweork's communication interrogative columns provides guidance on defining enterprise architecture. Please select answer(s) that is(are) coupled correctly:

Question Type

multi-select

Answer 1

What -> The inventory Column

Answer 2

What -> The entity column

Answer 3

When -> The timing column

Answer 4

Why -> The motivation column

Answer 5

Who -> The responsibility column

Answer 6

How -> The process column

Correct Response

1,3,4,5,6

Explanation

Please refer to page 103 of DMBOK2.

Knowledge Area

Data Architecture

Question 12

What model is the highest level model within the enterprise data model?

Question Type

multiple-choice

Answer 1

Logical model

Answer 2

Physical model

Answer 3

Conceptual model

Answer 4

Subject Area model

Correct Response

3

Explanation

Please refer to page 106 of DMBOK2.

Knowledge Area

Data Architecture

Question 13

For each subject area logical model: Decrease detail by adding attributes and less-significant entities and relationships.

Question Type

multiple-choice

Answer 1

True

Answer 2

False

Correct Response

2

Explanation

Please refer to page 106 of DMBOK2.

Knowledge Area

Data Architecture

Question 14

Data flows map and document relationships between data and:

Question Type

multi-select

Answer 1

Locations where local differences occur

Answer 2

Situations where local differences occur

Answer 3

Network segments

Answer 4

Applications within a business process

Answer 5

None of the above

Answer 6

All of the above

Correct Response

1,3,4

Explanation

Please refer to page 108 of DMBOK2.

Knowledge Area

Data Architecture

Question 15

Enterprise data architecture usually include the following work streams:

Question Type

multi-select

Answer 1

Strategy

Answer 2

Governance

Answer 3

Organization

Answer 4

Results

Answer 5

Working methods

Answer 6

All of the above

Question 16

A roadmap for enterprise data architecture describes the architecture's 3 to 5-year development path. The roadmap should be guided by a data management maturity assessment.

Question Type

multiple-choice

Answer 1

True

Answer 2

False

Question 17

Enterprise data architecture project-related activities include:

Question Type

multi-select

Answer 1

Define maturity assessment

Answer 2

Define scope

Answer 3

Design

Answer 4

Implement

Answer 5

None of the above

Answer 6

All of the above

Correct Response

2,3,4

Explanation

Please refer to page 113-114 of DMBOK2.

Knowledge Area

Data Architecture

Question 18

The process of building architectural activities into projects also differ between methodologies. They include:

Question Type

multi-select

Answer 1

Waterfall methods

Answer 2

Incremental methods

Answer 3

Kanban method

Answer 4

Agile iterative method

Answer 5

Duck and dive method

Answer 6

Pump and dump method

Question 19

Data modelling tools and model repositories are necessary for managing the enterprise data model in all levels.

Question Type

multiple-choice

Answer 1

True

Answer 2

False

Correct Response

1

Explanation

Please refer to page 115 of DMBOK2.

Knowledge Area

Data Architecture

Question 20

Characteristics that minimise distractions and maximise useful information include, but not limited to, consistent object attributes

Question Type

multiple-choice

Answer 1

True

Answer 2

False

Correct Response

1

Explanation

Please refer to page 82 of DMBOK2.

Knowledge Area

Data Architecture

Chapter 5

Question 1

A deliverable in the data modelling and design context diagram is the logical data model.

Question Type

multiple-choice

Answer 1

True

Answer 2

False

Correct Response

1

Explanation

Please refer to page 124 of DMBOK2.

Knowledge Area

Data Modelling and Design

Question 2

Inputs in the data modelling and design context diagram include:

Question Type

multi-select

Answer 1

Data standards

Answer 2

Data sets

Answer 3

Data Management Architecture

Answer 4

Systems Architecture

Answer 5

Data architecture

Answer 6

Enterprise taxonomy

Correct Response

1,2,5,6

Explanation

Please refer to page 124 of DMBOK2.

Knowledge Area

Data Modelling and Design

Question 3

Data models comprise and contain metadata essential to data consumers.

Question Type

multiple-choice

Answer 1

True

Answer 2

False

Correct Response

1

Explanation

Please refer to page 125 of DMBOK2.

Knowledge Area

Data Modelling and Design

Question 4

Data models are critical to effective management of data. They:

Question Type

multi-select

Answer 1

Provide a common vocabulary around data

Answer 2

Capture and document explicit knowledge about an organization's data and systems

Answer 3

Serve as a primary communication tool during projects

Answer 4

Provide the starting point for customizations, integration or even replacement of an application

Answer 5

Provide the organisation with clear system of the architecture

Answer 6

Make the integration between data management and data analytics possible

Correct Response

1,2,3,4

Explanation

Please refer to page 125 of DMBOK2.

Knowledge Area

Data Modelling and Design

Question 5

Confirming and documenting understanding of different perspectives facilitate:

Question Type

multi-select

Answer 1

Formalization

Answer 2

Normalization

Answer 3

Scope definition

Answer 4

Knowledge retention/documentation

Question 6

Data modelling is most infrequently performed in the context of systems and maintenance efforts, known as SDLC.

Question Type

multiple-choice

Answer 1

True

Answer 2

False

Correct Response

2

Explanation

Please refer to page 126 of DMBOK2.

Knowledge Area

Data Modelling and Design

Question 7

SDLC stands for:

Question Type

multiple-choice

Answer 1

System development leverage cycle

Answer 2

System design lifecycle

Answer 3

System and design long cycle

Answer 4

System development lifecycle

Correct Response

4

Explanation

Please refer to page 126 of DMBOK2.

Knowledge Area

Data Modelling and Design

Question 8

Category information is one of the types of data that can be modelled.

Question Type

multiple-choice

Answer 1

True

Answer 2

False

Correct Response

1

Explanation

Please refer to page 126 of DMBOK2.

Knowledge Area

Data Modelling and Design

Question 9

Business activity information is one of the types of data that can be modelled.

Question Type

multiple-choice

Answer 1

True

Answer 2

False

Correct Response

2

Explanation

Please refer to page 127 of DMBOK2.

Knowledge Area

Data Modelling and Design

Question 10

Examples of the 'Who' entity category include: employee; patient; player; and suspect.

Question Type

multiple-choice

Answer 1

True

Answer 2

False

Correct Response

1

Explanation

Please refer to page 127 of DMBOK2.

Knowledge Area

Data Modelling and Design

Question 11

Examples of the 'What' entity category include the following nouns:

Question Type

multi-select

Answer 1

Product

Answer 2

Service

Answer 3

Time

Answer 4

Sales amount

Answer 5

Payment quantity

Answer 6

All of the above

Correct Response

1,2

Explanation

Please refer to page 128 of DMBOK2.

Knowledge Area

Data Modelling and Design

Question 12

High quality data definition exhibit three characteristics:

Question Type

Multi-select

Answer 1

Clearness

Answer 2

Clarity

Answer 3

Accuracy

Answer 4

Completeness

Question 13

The number of entities in a relationship is the arity of the relationship. The most common are:

Question Type

multi-select

Answer 1

Unary

Answer 2

Binary

Answer 3

Trinary

Answer 4

Ternary

Correct Response

1,2,4

Explanation

Please refer to page 131 of DMBOK2.

Knowledge Area

Data Modelling and Design

Question 14

What type of key is used in physical and sometimes logical relational data modelling schemes to represent a relationship?

Question Type

multiple-choice

Answer 1

Primary key

Answer 2

Foreign key

Answer 3

Network key

Answer 4

Applications key

Answer 5

Door key

Answer 6

All of the above

Correct Response

2

Explanation

Please refer to page 132 of DMBOK2.

Knowledge Area

Data Modelling and Design

Question 15

Please select valid modelling schemes or notations

Question Type

multi-select

Answer 1

NoSQL

Answer 2

Dimensional

Answer 3

Relational

Answer 4

Object-orientated

Answer 5

Fact-based

Answer 6

Matrix-based

Question 16

Domains can be identified in different ways including: data type; data format; list; range; and rule-based.

Question Type

multiple-choice

Answer 1

True

Answer 2

False

Question 17

Snowflaking is the term given to normalizing the flat, single-table, dimensional structure in a star schema into the respective component hierarchical or network structures.

Question Type

multi-select

Answer 1

True

Answer 2

False

1

Explanation

Please refer to page 139 of DMBOK2.

Knowledge Area

Data Modelling and Design

Question 18

Class operations can be:

Question Type

multi-select

Answer 1

General: Hidden

Answer 2

Public: Externally visible

Answer 3

Internally visible: Visible to children objects

Answer 4

Private: Hidden

Correct Response

2,3,4

Explanation

Please refer to page 141 of DMBOK2.

Knowledge Area

Data Modelling and Design

Question 19

The data-vault is an object-orientated, time-based and uniquely linked set of normalized tables that support one or more functional areas of business.

Question Type

multiple-choice

Answer 1

True

Answer 2

False

Correct Response

2

Explanation

Please refer to page 141 of DMBOK2.

Knowledge Area

Data Modelling and Design

Question 20

Time-based patterns are used when data values must be associated in chronological order and with specific time values.

Question Type

multiple-choice

Answer 1

True

Answer 2

False

Chapter 6

Question 1

Data Storage and Operations: The design, implementation and support of stored data to maximize its value.

Question Type

multiple-choice

Answer 1

True

Answer 2

False

Correct Response

1

Explanation

Please refer to page 170 of DMBOK2.

Knowledge Area

Data Storage and Operations

Question 2

Inputs in the data storage and operations context diagram include:

Question Type

multi-select

Answer 1

Data requirements

Answer 2

Service level agreements

Answer 3

Data Management Architecture

Answer 4

Systems Architecture

Answer 5

Data architecture

Answer 6

Data models

Correct Response

1,2,5,6

Explanation

Please refer to page 170 of DMBOK2.

Knowledge Area

Data Storage and Operations

Question 3

Companies do not rely on their information systems to run their operations.

Question Type

multiple-choice

Answer 1

True

Answer 2

False

Explanation

Please refer to page 171 of DMBOK2.

Knowledge Area

Data Storage and Operations

Question 4

The goals of data storage and operations include:

Question Type

multi-select

Answer 1

Managing performance of data assets

Answer 2

Capture and document explicit knowledge about an organization's data and systems

Answer 3

Managing the availability of data throughout the data lifecycle

Answer 4

Provide the starting point for customizations, integration or even replacement of an application

Answer 5

Managing the performance of data transactions

Answer 6

Make the integration between data management and data analytics possible

Correct Response

1,3,5

Explanation

Please refer to page 171 of DMBOK2.

Knowledge Area

Data Storage and Operations

Question 5

Please select correct term for the following sentence: Any collection of stored data regardless of structure or content. Some large databases refer to instances and schema.

Question Type

multiple-choice

Answer 1

Schema

Answer 2

Database

Answer 3

Node

Answer 4

Instance

Correct Response

2

Explanation

Please refer to page 172 of DMBOK2.

Knowledge Area

Data Storage and Operations

Question 6

A node is a group of computers hosting either processing or data as part of a distributed database.

Question Type

multiple-choice

Answer 1

True

Answer 2

False

Correct Response

2

Explanation

Please refer to page 172 of DMBOK2.

Knowledge Area

Data Storage and Operations

Question 7

SLA Stands for:

Question Type

multiple-choice

Answer 1

Service Level Agreement

Answer 2

System Lifecycle Audit

Answer 3

System Latitude Audit

Answer 4

Service Lifecycle Audit

Correct Response

1

Explanation

Please refer to page 170 of DMBOK2.

Knowledge Area

Data Storage and Operations

Question 8

The database administrator (DBA) is the most established and the most widely adopted data professional role.

Question Type

multiple-choice

Answer 1

True

Answer 2

False

Correct Response

1

Explanation

Please refer to page 173 of DMBOK2.

Knowledge Area

Data Storage and Operations

Question 9

DBAs exclusively perform all the activities of data storage and operations.

Question Type

multiple-choice

Answer 1

True

Answer 2

False

Correct Response

2

Explanation

Please refer to page 173 of DMBOK2.

Knowledge Area

Data Storage and Operations

Question 10

An application DBA leads the review and administration of procedural database objects.

Question Type

multiple-choice

Answer 1

True

Answer 2

False

2

Explanation

Please refer to page 174 of DMBOK2.

Knowledge Area

Data Storage and Operations

Question 11

Please select the types of DBA specializations:

Question Type

multi-select

Answer 1

Data

Answer 2

Application

Answer 3

Innovation

Answer 4

Development

Answer 5

Procedural

Answer 6

All of the above

Correct Response

2,4,5

Explanation

Please refer to page 173 of DMBOK2.

Knowledge Area

Data Storage and Operations

Question 12

Please select the two classifications of database types:

Question Type

Multi-select

Answer 1

Centralized

Answer 2

Generic

Answer 3

Distributed

Answer 4

MapReduce

Question 13

There are numerous methods of implementing databases on the cloud. The most common are:

Question Type

multi-select

Answer 1

Virtual machine image

Answer 2

Distributed machine image

Answer 3

DAAS

Answer 4

Managed database hosting on the cloud

Correct Response

1,3,4

Explanation

Please refer to page 178 of DMBOK2.

Knowledge Area

Data Storage and Operations

Question 14

The CAP theorem asserts that the distributed system cannot comply with all the parts of the ACID. A distributed system must instead trade-off between the following properties:

Question Type

multi-select

Answer 1

Consistency

Answer 2

Utilization

Answer 3

Availability

Answer 4

System development

Answer 5

Partition tolerance

Answer 6

All of the above

Correct Response

1,3,5

Explanation

Please refer to page 180 of DMBOK2.

Knowledge Area

Data Storage and Operations

Question 15

The acronym BASE is made up of:

Question Type

multi-select

Answer 1

Basically available

Answer 2

Basically not available

Answer 3

Software state

Answer 4

Soft state

Answer 5

Eventual consistency

Answer 6

Everything considered

Correct Response

1,4,5

Explanation

Please refer to page 179 of DMBOK2.

Knowledge Area

Data Storage and Operations

Question 16

The CAP theorem states that at most two of the three properties: consistency, availability and partition tolerance can exist in any shared data system.

Question Type

multiple-choice

Answer 1

True

Answer 2

False

Correct Response

1

Explanation

Please refer to page 180 of DMBOK2.

Knowledge Area

Data Storage and Operations

Question 17

SSD is the abbreviation for Solid State Dimension.

Question Type

multiple-choice

Answer 1

True

Answer 2

False

Correct Response

2

Explanation

Please refer to page 182 of DMBOK2.

Knowledge Area

Data Storage and Operations

Question 18

Test environments serve many uses:

Question Type

multi-select

Answer 1

Quality Assurance Testing (QA)

Answer 2

Integration Testing

Answer 3

User Acceptance Testing (UAT)

Answer 4

Performance Testing

Answer 5

All of the above

Answer 6

None of the above

Correct Response

5

Explanation

Please refer to page 183 of DMBOK2.

Knowledge Area

Data Storage and Operations

Question 19

A sandbox environment can either be a sub-set of the production system, walled off from production processing or a completely separate environment.

Question Type

multiple-choice

Answer 1

True

Answer 2

False

Correct Response

1

Explanation

Please refer to page 184 of DMBOK2.

Knowledge Area

Data Storage and Operations

Question 20

A sandbox is an alternate environment that allows write-only connections to production data and can be managed by the administrator.

Question Type

multiple-choice

Answer 1

True

Answer 2

False

Correct Response

2

Explanation

Please refer to page 184 of DMBOK2.

Knowledge Area

Data Storage and Operations

Chapter 7

Question 1

Data security includes the planning, development and execution of security policies and procedures to provide authentication, authorisation, access and auditing of data and information assets.

Question Type

multiple-choice

Answer 1

True

Answer 2

False

Correct Response

1

Explanation

Please refer to page 217 of DMBOK2.

Knowledge Area

Data Security

Question 2

The goals of data security practices is to protect information assets in alignment with privacy and confidentiality regulations, contractual agreements and business requirements. These requirements come from:

Question Type

multi-select

Answer 1

Stakeholders

Answer 2

Government regulations

Answer 3

Proprietary business concerns

Answer 4

Legitimate access needs

Answer 5

Contractual obligations

Answer 6

None of the above

Correct Response

1,2,3,4,5

Explanation

Please refer to page 217-218 of DMBOK2.

Knowledge Area

Data Security

Question 3

A deliverable in the data security context diagram is the data security architecture.

Question Type

multiple-choice

Answer 1

True

Answer 2

False

Question 4

The goals of data security include:

Question Type

multi-select

Answer 1

Managing performance of data assets

Answer 2

Enable appropriate access to enterprise data assets

Answer 3

Managing the availability of data throughout the data lifecycle

Answer 4

Understand and comply with all relevant regulations and policies for privacy and confidentiality

Answer 5

Managing the performance of data transactions

Answer 6

Ensure that the privacy and confidentiality needs of all stakeholders are enforced and audited

Correct Response

2,4,6

Explanation

Please refer to page 219 of DMBOK2.

Knowledge Area

Data Security

Question 5

What are the primary drivers of data security activities?

Question Type

multi-select

Answer 1

Risk reduction

Answer 2

Risk alleviation

Answer 3

Business growth

Answer 4

Business compliance

Correct Response

2,3

Explanation

Please refer to page 220 of DMBOK2.

Knowledge Area

Data Security

Question 6

Data security issues, breaches and unwarranted restrictions on employee access to data cannot directly impact operational success.

Question Type

multiple-choice

Answer 1

True

Answer 2

False

Question 7

Vulnerability is defined as:

Question Type

multiple-choice

Answer 1

a patch in a system that allows it to be successfully unpatched and compromised.

Answer 2

being highly data risk rated

Answer 3

a strength in a system that allows external stakeholders to view data records.

Answer 4

a weakness or defect in a system that allows it to be successfully attacked and compromised.

Correct Response

4

Explanation

Please refer to page 223 of DMBOK2.

Knowledge Area

Data Security

Question 8

Risk classifications describe the sensitivity of the data and the likelihood that it might be sought after for malicious purposes.

Question Type

multiple-choice

Answer 1

True

Answer 2

False

Correct Response

1

Explanation

Please refer to page 224 of DMBOK2.

Knowledge Area

Data Security

Question 9

Data integrity is the state of being partitioned – protected from being whole.

Question Type

multiple-choice

Answer 1

True

Answer 2

False

2

Explanation

Please refer to page 226 of DMBOK2.

Knowledge Area

Data Security

Question 10

The four A's in security processes include:

Question Type

multi-select

Answer 1

Audit

Answer 2

Authentication

Answer 3

Access

Answer 4

Authorization

Answer 5

Aliment

Answer 6

Applicable

Correct Response

1,2,3,4

Explanation

Please refer to page 225 of DMBOK2.

Knowledge Area

Data Security

Question 11

There are several methods for masking data:

Question Type

multi-select

Answer 1

Substitution

Answer 2

Temporal variance

Answer 3

Temporal stagnation

Answer 4

Value stagnation

Answer 5

Value variance

Answer 6

All of the above

Correct Response

1,2,5

Explanation

Please refer to page 228-229 of DMBOK2.

Knowledge Area

Data Security

Question 12

Please select the two concepts that drive security restrictions:

Question Type

Multi-select

Answer 1

Regulation

Answer 2

Regression

Answer 3

Confidence level

Answer 4

Confidentiality level

Correct Response

1,4

Explanation

Please refer to page 234-235 of DMBOK2.

Knowledge Area

Data Security

Question 13

Device security standards include:

Question Type

multi-select

Answer 1

Access policies regarding connections using mobile devices

Answer 2

Awareness of security vulnerabilities

Answer 3

Installation of malware software

Answer 4

Storage of data on fixed devices

Correct Response

1,2

Explanation

Please refer to page 233 of DMBOK2.

Knowledge Area

Data Security

Question 14

Confidentiality classification schemas might include two or more of the five confidentiality classification levels. Three correct classifications levels are:

Question Type

multi-select

Answer 1

Consistency

Answer 2

Internal use only

Answer 3

Restricted confidential

Answer 4

System development

Answer 5

Confidential

Answer 6

None of the above

Correct Response

2,3,5

Explanation

Please refer to page 235 of DMBOK2.

Knowledge Area

Data Security

Question 15

Malware types include:

Question Type

multi-select

Answer 1

Trojan horse

Answer 2

Worm

Answer 3

Weasel

Answer 4

Virus

Answer 5

Adware

Answer 6

Camware

Question 16

Malware refers to any infectious software created to damage, change or improperly access a computer or network.

Question Type

multiple-choice

Answer 1

True

Answer 2

False

Correct Response

1

Explanation

Please refer to page 242 of DMBOK2.

Knowledge Area

Data Security

Question 17

Instant Messaging (IM) allows a user to message each other in real-time.

Question Type

multiple-choice

Answer 1

True

Answer 2

False

Question 18

Different levels of policy are required to govern behavior to enterprise security. For example:

Question Type

multi-select

Answer 1

Data security policy

Answer 2

Business Security Policy

Answer 3

IT security policy

Answer 4

Enterprise security policy

Answer 5

All of the above

Answer 6

None of the above

Correct Response

1,3,4

Explanation

Please refer to page 247 of DMBOK2.

Knowledge Area

Data Security

Question 19

The IT security policy provides categories for individual application, database roles, user groups and information sensitivity.

Question Type

multiple-choice

Answer 1

True

Answer 2

False

Question 20

Data access control can be organized at an individual level or group level, depending on the need.

Question Type

multiple-choice

Answer 1

True

Answer 2

False

Correct Response

1

Explanation

Please refer to page 249 of DMBOK2.

Knowledge Area

Data Security

Chapter 8

Question 1

Data Integration and Interoperability (DII) describes processes related to the movement and consolidation of data within and between data stores, applications and organizations.

Question Type

multiple-choice

Answer 1

True

Answer 2

False

Correct Response

1

Explanation

Please refer to page 269 of DMBOK2.

Knowledge Area

Data Integration and Interoperability

Question 2

Data Integration and Interoperability is dependent on these other areas of data management:

Question Type

multi-select

Answer 1

Metadata

Answer 2

Data architecture

Answer 3

Data governance

Answer 4

Data security

Answer 5

Data modelling and design

Answer 6

Data storage and operations

Correct Response

1,2,3,4,5,6

Explanation

Please refer to page 270 of DMBOK2.

Knowledge Area

Data Integration and Interoperability

Question 3

The need to manage data movement efficiently is a primary driver for Data Integration and Interoperability.

Question Type

multiple-choice

Answer 1

True

Answer 2

False

Correct Response

1

Explanation

Please refer to page 270 of DMBOK2.

Knowledge Area

Data Integration and Interoperability

Question 4

The goals of Data Integration and Interoperability include:

Question Type

multi-select

Answer 1

Provide data securely, with regulatory compliance, in the format and timeframe needed.

Answer 2

Lower cost and complexity of managing solutions by developing shared models and interfaces.

Answer 3

Managing the availability of data throughout the data lifecycle

Answer 4

Provide the starting point for customizations, integration or even replacement of an application

Answer 5

Identify meaningful events and automatically trigger alerts and actions.

Answer 6

Support business intelligence, analytics, master data management and operational efficiency efforts.

Correct Response

1,2,5,6

Explanation

Please refer to page 271 of DMBOK2.

Knowledge Area

Data Integration and Interoperability

Question 5

One of the deliverables in the Data Integration and Interoperability context diagram is:

Question Type

multiple-choice

Answer 1

Data Integration and Interoperability Strategy

Answer 2

Data hogging

Answer 3

Data access agreements

Answer 4

Data security plan

Correct Response

3

Explanation

Please refer to page 271 of DMBOK2.

Knowledge Area

Data Integration and Interoperability

Question 6

ETL is the basic process which is central to all areas in Data Integration and Interoperability. It is an abbreviation for extract, transition and load.

Question Type

multiple-choice

Answer 1

True

Answer 2

False

Correct Response

2

Explanation

Please refer to page 273 of DMBOK2.

Knowledge Area

Data Integration and Interoperability

Question 7

On example of a transformation process in ETL is:

Question Type

multiple-choice

Answer 1

Re-ordering

Answer 2

Recording

Answer 3

Duping

Answer 4

Servicing

Correct Response

1

Explanation

Please refer to page 273-274 of DMBOK2.

Knowledge Area

Data Integration and Interoperability

Question 8

The load step of ETL is physically storing or presenting the results of the transformation in the target system.

Question Type

multiple-choice

Answer 1

True

Answer 2

False

Question 9

A synonym for transformation in ETL is mapping. Mapping is the process of developing the lookup matrix from source to target structures, but not the result of the process.

Question Type

multiple-choice

Answer 1

True

Answer 2

False

Correct Response

2

Explanation

Please refer to page 275 of DMBOK2.

Knowledge Area

Data Integration and Interoperability

Question 10

Change Data Capture is a method of reducing bandwidth by filtering to include only data that has been changed within a defined timeframe.

Question Type

multiple-choice

Answer 1

True

Answer 2

False

Correct Response

1

Explanation

Please refer to page 275 of DMBOK2.

Knowledge Area

Data Integration and Interoperability

Question 11

There are three techniques for data-based change data capture, namely:

Question Type

multi-select

Answer 1

The source system populates specific data elements.

Answer 2

Application automated interfaces

Answer 3

The source system processes copy data that has changed into a separate object as part of the transaction, which is then used for the extract process.

Answer 4

The source systems send binary code through ASCI that makes the process rapid.

Answer 5

The source system processes add to a simple list of objects and identifiers when changing data, which is then used to control selection of data extraction.

Answer 6

None of the above

Correct Response

1,3,5

Explanation

Please refer to page 276 of DMBOK2.

Knowledge Area

Data Integration and Interoperability

Question 12

Latency can be:

Question Type

Multi-select

Answer 1

Batch

Answer 2

Event-driven

Answer 3

Distributed

Answer 4

Real-time synchronous

Correct Response

1,3,4

Explanation

Please refer to page 275 of DMBOK2.

Knowledge Area

Data Integration and Interoperability

Question 13

Examples of interaction models include:

Question Type

multi-select

Answer 1

Hub-and-spoke

Answer 2

Publish - subscribe

Answer 3

Point-to-point

Answer 4

Wheel-and-spike

Correct Response

1,2,3

Explanation

Please refer to page 280-281 of DMBOK2.

Knowledge Area

Data Integration and Interoperability

Question 14

As an often-overlooked aspects of basic data movement architecture, Process controls include:

Question Type

multi-select

Answer 1

Consistency logging

Answer 2

Exception logs

Answer 3

Database activity logs

Answer 4

Alerts

Answer 5

Exception logs

Answer 6

All of the above

Correct Response

2,3,4,5

Explanation

Please refer to page 282 of DMBOK2.

Knowledge Area

Data Integration and Interoperability

Question 15

Use business rules to support Data Integration and Interoperability at various points, to:

Question Type

multi-select

Answer 1

Direct the flow of data in the organization

Answer 2

Monitor the organization's operational data

Answer 3

Software alerts when events are triggered

Answer 4

Direct when to automatically trigger events and alerts

Answer 5

Consistency in allocation event resources

Answer 6

None of the above

Correct Response

1,2,4

Explanation

Please refer to page 289 of DMBOK2.

Knowledge Area

Data Integration and Interoperability

Question 16

The flow of data in a data integration solution does not have to be designed and documented.

Question Type

multiple-choice

Answer 1

True

Answer 2

False

Correct Response

2

Explanation

Please refer to page 291 of DMBOK2.

Knowledge Area

Data Integration and Interoperability

Question 17

Preparation and pre-processing of historical data needed in a predictive model may be performed in nightly batch processes or in near real-time.

Question Type

multiple-choice

Answer 1

True

Answer 2

False

Question 18

Developing complex event processing solutions require:

Question Type

multi-select

Answer 1

Preparation of historical data and pre-population of a predictive model

Answer 2

Integration testing for subsequent logging requirements

Answer 3

Processing of real-time data stream to fully populate a predictive model and identify meaningful events

Answer 4

Executing the triggered action in response to the prediction

Answer 5

All of the above

Answer 6

None of the above

Correct Response

1,3,4

Explanation

Please refer to page 292 of DMBOK2.

Knowledge Area

Data Integration and Interoperability

Question 19

Real-time data integration is usually triggered by batch processing, such as historic data.

Question Type

multiple-choice

Answer 1

True

Answer 2

False

Correct Response

2

Explanation

Please refer to page 291 of DMBOK2.

Knowledge Area

Data Integration and Interoperability

Question 20

Integration of ETL data flows will usually be developed within tools specialised to manage those flows in a proprietary way.

Question Type

multiple-choice

Answer 1

True

Answer 2

False

Correct Response

1

Explanation

Please refer to page 291 of DMBOK2.

Knowledge Area

Data Integration and Interoperability

Chapter 9

Question 1

E-discovery is the process of finding electronic records that might serve as evidence in a legal action.

Question Type

multiple-choice

Answer 1

True

Answer 2

False

Correct Response

1

Explanation

Please refer to page 305 of DMBOK2.

Knowledge Area

Document and content management

Question 2

Deliverables in the document and content management context diagram include:

Question Type

multi-select

Answer 1

Metadata and reference data

Answer 2

Policy and procedure

Answer 3

Data governance

Answer 4

Content and records management strategy

Answer 5

Audit trail and log

Answer 6

Data storage and operations

Correct Response

2,3,4,5

Explanation

Please refer to page 304 of DMBOK2.

Knowledge Area

Document and content management

Question 3

Document and content management is defined as planning, implementation and control activities for storage management of data and information found in any form or medium.

Question Type

multiple-choice

Answer 1

True

Answer 2

False

Question 4

The goals of implementing best practices around document and content management include:

Question Type

multi-select

Answer 1

Ensuring effective and efficient retrieval and use of data and information in unstructured formats

Answer 2

Ensuring integration capabilities between structured and unstructured data

Answer 3

Complying with legal obligations and customer expectations

Answer 4

Enduring integration competencies between semi-structured systems

Answer 5

Managing the performance of data transactions

Answer 6

Make the integration between data management and data analytics possible

Question 5

Please select correct term for the following sentence: An organization shall assign a senior executive to appropriate individuals, adopt policies and processes to guide staff and ensure program audibility.

Question Type

multiple-choice

Answer 1

Principle of integrity

Answer 2

Principle of availability

Answer 3

Principle of retention

Answer 4

Principle of accountability

Correct Response

4

Explanation

Please refer to page 306 of DMBOK2.

Knowledge Area

Document and content management

Question 6

Content refers to the data and information inside a file, document or website.

Question Type

multiple-choice

Answer 1

True

Answer 2

False

Correct Response

1

Explanation

Please refer to page 307 of DMBOK2.

Knowledge Area

Document and content management

Question 7

ECM is an abbreviation for:

Question Type

multiple-choice

Answer 1

Enterprise compliance management

Answer 2

Enterprise compliance manager

Answer 3

Enterprise component management

Answer 4

Enterprise content management

Correct Response

4

Explanation

Please refer to page 307 of DMBOK2.

Knowledge Area

Document and content management

Question 8

Content management includes the systems for organizing information resources so that they can specially be stored.

Question Type

multiple-choice

Answer 1

True

Answer 2

False

Question 9

Content needs to be modular, structured, reusable and device and platform independent.

Question Type

multiple-choice

Answer 1

True

Answer 2

False

Correct Response

1

Explanation

Please refer to page 308 of DMBOK2.

Knowledge Area

Document and content management

Question 10

A controlled vocabulary is a defined list of explicitly allowed terms used to index, categorize, tag, sort and retrieve content through browsing and searching.

Question Type

multiple-choice

Answer 1

True

Answer 2

False

Correct Response

1

Explanation

Please refer to page 309 of DMBOK2.

Knowledge Area

Document and content management

Question 11

Taxonomies can have different structures, including:

Question Type

multi-select

Answer 1

Polyhierarchy

Answer 2

Application

Answer 3

Facet taxonomy

Answer 4

Network taxonomy

Answer 5

Flat taxonomy

Answer 6

All of the above

Correct Response

1,3,4,5

Explanation

Please refer to page 312-313 of DMBOK2.

Knowledge Area

Document and content management

Question 12

Well prepared records have characteristics such as:

Question Type

Multi-select

Answer 1

Context

Answer 2

Content

Answer 3

Compliance

Answer 4

Timeliness

Question 13

Information architecture is the process of creating structure for a body of information or content. It includes the following components:

Question Type

multi-select

Answer 1

Navigation maps

Answer 2

User flows

Answer 3

Use cases

Answer 4

Controlled technologies

Correct Response

1,2,3

Explanation

Please refer to page 320 of DMBOK2.

Knowledge Area

Document and content management

Question 14

Most document programs have policies related to:

Question Type

multi-select

Answer 1

Scope and compliance audits

Answer 2

Proper destruction of records

Answer 3

Proper construction of records

Answer 4

Identification and protection of vital records

Answer 5

Partition tolerance

Answer 6

All of the above

Correct Response

1,2,4

Explanation

Please refer to page 324 of DMBOK2.

Knowledge Area

Document and content management

Question 15

ANSI standard 859 has three levels of control of data, based on the criticality of the data and the perceived harm that would occur if data were corrupt or otherwise unavailable, including:

Question Type

multi-select

Answer 1

Basic

Answer 2

Formal

Answer 3

Informal

Answer 4

Custody

Answer 5

Revision

Answer 6

None of the above

Question 16

A content strategy should end with an inventory of current state and a gap assessment.

Question Type

multiple-choice

Answer 1

True

Answer 2

False

Correct Response

2

Explanation

Please refer to page 324 of DMBOK2.

Knowledge Area

Document and content management

Question 17

Record management starts with a vague definition of what constitutes a record.

Question Type

multiple-choice

Answer 1

True

Answer 2

False

Correct Response

2

Explanation

Please refer to page 323 of DMBOK2.

Knowledge Area

Document and content management

Question 18

Some document management systems have a module that may support different types of workflows such as:

Question Type

multi-select

Answer 1

Quality Assurance Testing (QA)

Answer 2

Manual workflows that indicate where the user send the document

Answer 3

User Acceptance Testing (UAT)

Answer 4

Dynamic rules that allow for different workflows based on content

Answer 5

All of the above

Answer 6

None of the above

Correct Response

2,4

Explanation

Please refer to page 331 of DMBOK2.

Knowledge Area

Document and content management

Question 19

An image processing system captures, transforms and manages images of paper and electronic documents.

Question Type

multiple-choice

Answer 1

True

Answer 2

False

Correct Response

1

Explanation

Please refer to page 331 of DMBOK2.

Knowledge Area

Document and content management

Question 20

OCR is the abbreviation for Optical Character Recognition.

Question Type

multiple-choice

Answer 1

True

Answer 2

False

Explanation

Please refer to page 332 of DMBOK2.

Knowledge Area

Document and content management

Chapter 10

Question 1

Reference and Master data definition: Managing shared data to meet organizational goals, reduce risks associated with data redundancy, ensure higher quality, and reduce the costs of data integration.

Question Type

multiple-choice

Answer 1

True

Answer 2

False

Correct Response

1

Explanation

Please refer to page 348 of DMBOK2.

Knowledge Area

Reference and master data

Question 2

The most common drivers for initiating a Mater Data Management Program are:

Question Type

multi-select

Answer 1

Metadata insecurity

Answer 2

Managing data quality

Answer 3

Reducing risk

Answer 4

Managing the costs of data integration

Answer 5

Meeting organizational data requirements

Answer 6

Reducing latency

Correct Response

2,3,4,5

Explanation

Please refer to page 349 of DMBOK2.

Knowledge Area

Reference and master data

Question 3

A goal of reference and master data is to provide authoritative source of reconciled and quality-assessed master and reference data.

Question Type

multiple-choice

Answer 1

True

Answer 2

False

Correct Response

1

Explanation

Please refer to page 348 of DMBOK2.

Knowledge Area

Reference and master data

Question 4

Reference and Master Data Management follow these guiding principles:

Question Type

multi-select

Answer 1

Quality

Answer 2

Stewardship

Answer 3

Authority

Answer 4

Ownership

Answer 5

Exclusivity

Answer 6

Inclusivity

Correct Response

1,2,3,4

Explanation

Please refer to page 350 of DMBOK2.

Knowledge Area

Reference and master data

Question 5

Master data is an aggregation of:

Question Type

multi-select

Answer 1

Transaction Structure Data

Answer 2

Database Structure Data

Answer 3

Reference Data

Answer 4

Enterprise Structure Data

Correct Response

1,3,4

Explanation

Please refer to page 350-351 of DMBOK2.

Knowledge Area

Reference and master data

Question 6

Reference data management entails the preventative maintenance of undefined domain values, definitions and the relationship within and across domain values.

Question Type

multiple-choice

Answer 1

True

Answer 2

False

Explanation

Please refer to page 353 of DMBOK2.

Knowledge Area

Reference and master data

Question 7

SOR Stands for:

Question Type

multiple-choice

Answer 1

Service of Record

Answer 2

System of Record

Answer 3

System on Record

Answer 4

Service over Record

Correct Response

2

Explanation

Please refer to page 358 of DMBOK2.

Knowledge Area

Reference and master data

Question 8

A *System of Reference* is an authoritative system where data consumers can obtain reliable data to support transactions and analysis, even if the information did not originate in the system reference.

Question Type

multiple-choice

Answer 1

True

Answer 2

False

Correct Response

1

Explanation

Please refer to page 358 of DMBOK2.

Knowledge Area

Reference and master data

Question 9

A 'Golden Record' means that it is always a 100% complete and accurate representation of all entities within the organization.

Question Type

multiple-choice

Answer 1

True

Answer 2

False

Correct Response

2

Explanation

Please refer to page 359 of DMBOK2.

Knowledge Area

Reference and master data

Question 10

Master data management includes several basic steps, which include: Develop rules for accurately matching and merging entity instances.

Question Type

multiple-choice

Answer 1

True

Answer 2

False

Explanation

Please refer to page 360 of DMBOK2.

Knowledge Area

Reference and master data

Question 11

Data preparation for

Question Type

multi-select

Answer 1

Realistic

Answer 2

Opportunistic

Answer 3

Deterministic

Answer 4

Probabilistic

Answer 5

Procedural

Answer 6

All of the above

3,4

Explanation

Please refer to page 363 of DMBOK2.

Knowledge Area

Reference and master data

Question 12

Two risks with the Matching process are:

Question Type

Multi-select

Answer 1

False positives

Answer 2

False Certainties

Answer 3

False Negatives

Answer 4

False Uncertainties

Question 13

Consistent input data reduces the chance of errors in associating records. Preparation processes include:

Question Type

multi-select

Answer 1

Standardization

Answer 2

Enrichment

Answer 3

Validation

Answer 4

Database management

Correct Response

1,2,3

Explanation

Please refer to page 362 of DMBOK2.

Knowledge Area

Reference and master data

Question 14

Match rules for different scenarios require different workflows, including:

Question Type

multi-select

Answer 1

Consistency rules

Answer 2

Duplicate identification match rules

Answer 3

Match-merge rules

Answer 4

Match-split rules

Answer 5

Match-link rules

Answer 6

All of the above

Correct Response

2,3,5

Explanation

Please refer to page 364-365 of DMBOK2.

Knowledge Area

Reference and master data

Question 15

There are three basic approaches to implementing a Master Data hub environment, including:

Question Type

multi-select

Answer 1

Transaction hub

Answer 2

Distributed hub

Answer 3

Registry

Answer 4

Consolidated approach

Answer 5

Eventual consistency

Answer 6

Transparent hub

Correct Response

1,3,4

Explanation

Please refer to page 371-372 of DMBOK2.

Knowledge Area

Reference and master data

Question 16

A Global ID is the MDM solution-assigned and maintained unique identifier attached to reconciled records.

Question Type

multiple-choice

Answer 1

True

Answer 2

False

Correct Response

1

Explanation

Please refer to page 365 of DMBOK2.

Knowledge Area

Reference and master data

Question 17

Customer relationship management systems manage Master Data about customers.

Question Type

multiple-choice

Answer 1

True

Answer 2

False

Explanation

Please refer to page 366 of DMBOK2.

Knowledge Area

Reference and master data

Question 18

Key processing steps for MDM include:

Question Type

multi-select

Answer 1

Data model management

Answer 2

Data acquisition

Answer 3

Data validation, standardization and enrichment

Answer 4

Entity resolution

Answer 5

Data sharing and stewardship

Answer 6

None of the above

Correct Response

1,2,3,4,5

Explanation

Please refer to page 361 of DMBOK2.

Knowledge Area

Reference and master data

Question 19

In matching, false positives are three references that do not represent the same entity are linked with a single identifier.

Question Type

multiple-choice

Answer 1

True

Answer 2

False

Correct Response

2

Explanation

Please refer to page 363 of DMBOK2.

Knowledge Area

Reference and master data

Question 20

Product Master data can only focus on an organization's internal product and services.

Question Type

multiple-choice

Answer 1

True

Answer 2

False

Correct Response

2

Explanation

Please refer to page 367 of DMBOK2.

Knowledge Area

Reference and master data

Chapter 11

Question 1

Business requirements is an input in the Data Warehouse and Business Intelligence context diagram.

Question Type

multiple-choice

Answer 1

True

Answer 2

False

Correct Response

1

Explanation

Please refer to page 382 of DMBOK2.

Knowledge Area

Data warehouse and business intelligence

Question 2

Primary deliverables of the Data Warehouse and Business Intelligence context diagram include:

Question Type

multi-select

Answer 1

Data Products

Answer 2

Data Stewardship

Answer 3

Governance Activities

Answer 4

Release Plan

Answer 5

Load Tuning Activities

Answer 6

BI Activity Monitoring

Question 3

A goal of Data warehouse and business intelligence is to support and enable ineffective business analysis and decision making by knowledge workers.

Question Type

multiple-choice

Answer 1

True

Answer 2

False

Correct Response

2

Explanation

Please refer to page 382 of DMBOK2.

Knowledge Area

Data warehouse and business intelligence

Question 4

The implementation of a Data Warehouse should follow these guiding principles:

Question Type

multi-select

Answer 1

Managing performance of data assets

Answer 2

Focus on the business goals

Answer 3

Managing the availability of data throughout the data lifecycle

Answer 4

Start with the end in mind

Answer 5

Managing the performance of data transactions

Answer 6

Collaborate

Question 5

The difference between warehouses and operational systems do not include the following element:

Question Type

multiple-choice

Answer 1

Time variant

Answer 2

Database

Answer 3

Subject-orientated

Answer 4

Historical

Correct Response

2

Explanation

Please refer to page 386 of DMBOK2.

Knowledge Area

Data warehouse and business intelligence

Question 6

Data warehousing describes the operational extract, cleaning, transformation, control and load processes that maintain the data in a data warehouse.

Question Type

multiple-choice

Answer 1

True

Answer 2

False

Correct Response

1

Explanation

Please refer to page 385 of DMBOK2.

Knowledge Area

Data warehouse and business intelligence

Question 7

CIF stands for:

Question Type

multiple-choice

Answer 1

Company Information Factory

Answer 2

Corporate Information Floor

Answer 3

Corporate Information Factories

Answer 4

Corporate Information Factory

Correct Response

4

Explanation

Please refer to page 386 of DMBOK2.

Knowledge Area

Data warehouse and business intelligence

Question 8

The data in Data warehouses and marts differ. Data is organized by subject rather than function

Question Type

multiple-choice

Answer 1

True

Answer 2

False

Correct Response

1

Explanation

Please refer to page 387 of DMBOK2.

Knowledge Area

Data warehouse and business intelligence

Question 9

An Operational Data Mart is a data mart focused on tactical decision support.

Question Type

multiple-choice

Answer 1

True

Answer 2

False

Correct Response

1

Explanation

Please refer to page 387 of DMBOK2.

Knowledge Area

Data warehouse and business intelligence

Question 10

Operational reports are outputs from the data stewards.

Question Type

multiple-choice

Answer 1

True

Answer 2

False

Correct Response

2

Explanation

Please refer to page 387 of DMBOK2.

Knowledge Area

Data warehouse and business intelligence

Question 11

The Data Warehouse encompasses all components in the data staging and data presentation areas, including:

Question Type

multi-select

Answer 1

Data Access Tool

Answer 2

Application Tool

Answer 3

Operational source systems

Answer 4

Data staging area

Answer 5

Data presentation area

Answer 6

All of the above

Correct Response

1,3,4,5

Explanation

Please refer to page 389 of DMBOK2.

Knowledge Area

Data warehouse and business intelligence

Question 12

The Data Warehouse has a set of storage areas, including:

Question Type

Multi-select

Answer 1

Staging areas

Answer 2

Data marts

Answer 3

Cubes

Answer 4

Kubernetes

Correct Response

1,2,3

Explanation

Please refer to page 391-392 of DMBOK2.

Knowledge Area

Data warehouse and business intelligence

Question 13

The impact of the changes from new volatile data must be isolated from the bulk of the historical, non-volatile DW data. There are three main approaches, including:

Question Type

multi-select

Answer 1

Streaming

Answer 2

Messaging

Answer 3

DAAS

Answer 4

Trickle Feeds

Correct Response

1,2,4

Explanation

Please refer to page 394 of DMBOK2.

Knowledge Area

Data warehouse and business intelligence

Question 14

Typically, DW/BI have three concurrent development tracks:

Question Type

multi-select

Answer 1

Data mart

Answer 2

Business Intelligence tools

Answer 3

Data

Answer 4

System development

Answer 5

Techonology

Answer 6

None of the above

Correct Response

2,3,5

Explanation

Please refer to page 396 of DMBOK2.

Knowledge Area

Data warehouse and business intelligence

Question 15

Business Intelligence tool types include:

Question Type

multi-select

Answer 1

Technology reporting

Answer 2

Operational reporting

Answer 3

Descriptive, self-service analytics

Answer 4

Operations performance management (OPM)

Answer 5

Business performance management (BPM)

Answer 6

Predictive, self-service analytics

Correct Response

2,3,5

Explanation

Please refer to page 404 of DMBOK2.

Knowledge Area

Data warehouse and business intelligence

Question 16

An implemented warehouse and its customer facing BI tool is a data product.

Question Type

multiple-choice

Answer 1

True

Answer 2

False

Correct Response

1

Explanation

Please refer to page 399 of DMBOK2.

Knowledge Area

Data warehouse and business intelligence

Question 17

Release management is critical to batch development processes that grows new capabilities.

Question Type

multiple-choice

Answer 1

True

Answer 2

False

Correct Response

2

Explanation

Please refer to page 399 of DMBOK2.

Knowledge Area

Data warehouse and business intelligence

Question 18

Three classic implementation approaches that support Online Analytical Processing include:

Question Type

multi-select

Answer 1

QOLAP

Answer 2

ROLAP

Answer 3

OLAP2

Answer 4

HOLAP

Answer 5

MOLAP

Answer 6

None of the above

Correct Response

2,4,5

Explanation

Please refer to page 407 of DMBOK2.

Knowledge Area

Data warehouse and business intelligence

Question 19

Self-service is a fundamental delivery channel in the BI portfolio.

Question Type

multiple-choice

Answer 1

True

Answer 2

False

Correct Response

1

Explanation

Please refer to page 408 of DMBOK2.

Knowledge Area

Data warehouse and business intelligence

Question 20

A data dictionary is necessary to support the use of a DW.

Question Type

multiple-choice

Answer 1

True

Answer 2

False

Correct Response

1

Explanation

Please refer to page 402 of DMBOK2.

Knowledge Area

Data warehouse and business intelligence

Chapter 12

Question 1

With reliable Metadata an organization does not know what data it has, what the data represents and how it moves through the systems, who has access to it, or what it means for the data to be of high quality.

Question Type

multiple-choice

Answer 1

True

Answer 2

False

Correct Response

2

Explanation

Please refer to page 418 of DMBOK2.

Knowledge Area

Metadata management

Question 2

Deliverables in the Metadata Management context diagram include:

Question Type

multi-select

Answer 1

Metadata Strategy

Answer 2

Metadata Standards

Answer 3

Data Lineage

Answer 4

Metadata Architecture

Answer 5

Metadata design

Answer 6

Data storage and operations

Question 3

Poorly managed Metadata leads to, among other, redundant data and data management processes.

Question Type

multiple-choice

Answer 1

True

Answer 2

False

Correct Response

1

Explanation

Please refer to page 420 of DMBOK2.

Knowledge Area

Metadata management

Question 4

The goals of Metadata management include:

Question Type

multi-select

Answer 1

Managing performance of data assets

Answer 2

Ensure metadata quality, consistency, currency and security

Answer 3

Managing the availability of data throughout the data lifecycle

Answer 4

Provide standard ways to make metadata accessible to metadata consumers

Answer 5

Managing the performance of data transactions

Answer 6

Establish or enforce the use of technical Metadata standards to enable data exchange

Correct Response

2,4,6

Explanation

Please refer to page 420-421 of DMBOK2.

Knowledge Area

Metadata management

Question 5

Metadata is described using a different set of categories, not including:

Question Type

multiple-choice

Answer 1

Descriptive metadata

Answer 2

Database metadata

Answer 3

Structural metadata

Answer 4

Administrative metadata

Correct Response

2

Explanation

Please refer to page 422 of DMBOK2.

Knowledge Area

Metadata management

Question 6

Business metadata focuses largely on the content and condition of the data and includes details related to data governance.

Question Type

multiple-choice

Answer 1

True

Answer 2

False

Correct Response

1

Explanation

Please refer to page 422 of DMBOK2.

Knowledge Area

Metadata management

Question 7

Operational Metadata describes details of the processing and accessing of data. Which one is not an example:

Question Type

multiple-choice

Answer 1

Error logs

Answer 2

Schedule anomalies

Answer 3

Purge criteria

Answer 4

Failure logs

Correct Response

4

Explanation

Please refer to page 423-424 of DMBOK2.

Knowledge Area

Metadata management

Question 8

Technical Metadata provides data about the technical data, the systems that store data, and the processes that move between systems.

Question Type

multiple-choice

Answer 1

True

Answer 2

False

Correct Response

2

Explanation

Please refer to page 423 of DMBOK2.

Knowledge Area

Metadata management

Question 9

Metadata is essential to the management of unstructured data as it id to the management of structured data.

Question Type

multiple-choice

Answer 1

True

Answer 2

False

Correct Response

1

Explanation

Please refer to page 424 of DMBOK2.

Knowledge Area

Metadata management

Question 10

The minority of operational metadata is generated as data is processed.

Question Type

multiple-choice

Answer 1

True

Answer 2

False

Correct Response

2

Explanation

Please refer to page 425 of DMBOK2.

Knowledge Area

Metadata management

Question 11

The business glossary application is structured to meet the functional requirements of the three core audiences:

Question Type

multi-select

Answer 1

Data users

Answer 2

Application users

Answer 3

Innovation users

Answer 4

Business users

Answer 5

Data stewards

Answer 6

Technical users

Correct Response

4,5,6

Explanation

Please refer to page 426-427 of DMBOK2.

Knowledge Area

Metadata management

Question 12

Examples of business metadata include:

Question Type

Multi-select

Answer 1

Data models

Answer 2

Data quality rules

Answer 3

Data usage notes

Answer 4

Data Standards

Correct Response

1,2,3,4

Explanation

Please refer to page 423 of DMBOK2.

Knowledge Area

Metadata management

Question 13

Examples of technical metadata include:

Question Type

multi-select

Answer 1

Access permission

Answer 2

Recovery and backup rules

Answer 3

Colum properties

Answer 4

Data subject properties

Correct Response

1,2,3

Explanation

Please refer to page 423 of DMBOK2.

Knowledge Area

Metadata management

Question 14

The business glossary should capture business terms attributes such as:

Question Type

multi-select

Answer 1

Lineage

Answer 2

Utilization

Answer 3

Common misunderstanding in terms

Answer 4

System development

Answer 5

Algorithms to supporting definitions

Answer 6

All of the above

Correct Response

1,3,5

Explanation

Please refer to page 427 of DMBOK2.

Knowledge Area

Metadata management

Question 15

The acronym CMDB stands for:

Question Type

multiple-choice

Answer 1

Customization management tools or databases

Answer 2

Classic management technologies or databases

Answer 3

Cached management technologies or databases

Answer 4

Configuration management tools or databases

Answer 5

Cached management tools or databases

Answer 6

Classic monitoring technologies or databases

Correct Response

4

Explanation

Please refer to page 427 of DMBOK2.

Knowledge Area

Metadata management

Question 16

CMDB provide the capability to manage and maintain Metdata specifically related to the IT assets, the relationships among them, and contractual details of the assets.

Question Type

multiple-choice

Answer 1

True

Answer 2

False

Correct Response

1

Explanation

Please refer to page 427 of DMBOK2.

Knowledge Area

Metadata management

Question 17

SOA stand for Service Orchestrated Architecture

Question Type

multiple-choice

Answer 1

True

Answer 2

False

Correct Response

2

Explanation

Please refer to page 430 of DMBOK2.

Knowledge Area

Metadata management

Question 18

All metadata management solutions include architectural layers including:

Question Type

multi-select

Answer 1

Metadata Quality Assurance Testing

Answer 2

Metadata integration

Answer 3

Metadata usage

Answer 4

Metadata delivery

Answer 5

Metadata control and management

Answer 6

None of the above

Correct Response

2,3,4,5

Explanation

Please refer to page 431 of DMBOK2.

Knowledge Area

Metadata management

Question 19

An advantage of a centralized repository include: High availability since it is independent of the source systems.

Question Type

multiple-choice

Answer 1

True

Answer 2

False

Correct Response

1

Explanation

Please refer to page 431 of DMBOK2.

Knowledge Area

Metadata management

Question 20

A limitation of the centralized approach include: Maintenance of a decentralized repository is costly.

Question Type

multiple-choice

Answer 1

True

Answer 2

False

Correct Response

2

Explanation

Please refer to page 431 of DMBOK2.

Knowledge Area

Metadata management

Chapter 13

Question 1

Effective data management involves a set of complex, interrelated processes that enable an organisation to use its data to achieve strategic goals.

Question Type

multiple-choice

Answer 1

True

Answer 2

False

Correct Response

1

Explanation

Please refer to page 449 of DMBOK2.

Knowledge Area

Data quality

Question 2

Deliverables in the data quality context diagram include:

Question Type

multi-select

Answer 1

DQM Procedures

Answer 2

Data architecture

Answer 3

Data governance

Answer 4

DQ Policies and guidelines

Answer 5

Analyses from data profiling

Answer 6

Data quality Service Level Agreements

Correct Response

1,4,5,6

Explanation

Please refer to page 451 of DMBOK2.

Knowledge Area

Data quality

Question 3

The term data quality refers to only the characteristics associated with high quality data.

Question Type

multiple-choice

Answer 1

True

Answer 2

False

Question 4

Data can be assessed based on whether it is required by:

Question Type

multi-select

Answer 1

Regulatory reporting

Answer 2

Capturing policy

Answer 3

Ongoing operations

Answer 4

Provide the starting point for customizations, integration or even replacement of an application

Answer 5

Business policy

Answer 6

Make the integration between data management and data analytics possible

Correct Response

1,3,5

Explanation

Please refer to page 454 of DMBOK2.

Knowledge Area

Data quality

Question 5

Please select the incorrect item that does not represent a dimension in the Data Values category in *Data Quality for the Information age.*

Question Type

multiple-choice

Answer 1

Currency

Answer 2

Timeliness

Answer 3

Consistency

Answer 4

Completeness

Correct Response

2

Explanation

Please refer to page 455-456 of DMBOK2.

Knowledge Area

Data quality

Question 6

The accuracy dimension of data quality refers to the degree that data correctly respresents 'real-life' entities.

Question Type

multiple-choice

Answer 1

True

Answer 2

False

Correct Response

1

Explanation

Please refer to page 458 of DMBOK2.

Knowledge Area

Data quality

Question 7

What ISO standard defines characteristics that can be tested by any organisation in the data supply chain to objectively determine conformance of the data to this ISO standard.

Question Type

multiple-choice

Answer 1

ISO 9000

Answer 2

ISO 7000

Answer 3

ISO 8000

Answer 4

ISO 9001

Correct Response

3

Explanation

Please refer to page 461 of DMBOK2.

Knowledge Area

Data quality

Question 8

The accuracy dimension has to do with the precision of data values.

Question Type

multiple-choice

Answer 1

True

Answer 2

False

Correct Response

1

Explanation

Please refer to page 460 of DMBOK2.

Knowledge Area

Data quality

Question 9

Data Integrity includes ideas associated with completeness, accuracy, and consistency.

Question Type

multiple-choice

Answer 1

True

Answer 2

False

Question 10

Validity, as a dimension of data quality, refers to whether data values are consistent with a defined domain of values.

Question Type

multiple-choice

Answer 1

True

Answer 2

False

Correct Response

1

Explanation

Please refer to page 459 of DMBOK2.

Knowledge Area

Data quality

Question 11

Dimensions of data quality include:

Question Type

multi-select

Answer 1

Validity

Answer 2

Privacy

Answer 3

Innovation

Answer 4

Accessibility

Answer 5

Currency

Answer 6

All of the above

Correct Response

1,2,4,5

Explanation

Please refer to page 460 of DMBOK2.

Knowledge Area

Data quality

Question 12

ISO 8000 will describe the structure and the organization of data quality management, including:

Question Type

Multi-select

Answer 1

Data Quality Availability

Answer 2

Data Quality Planning

Answer 3

Data Quality Control

Answer 4

Data Quality Assurance

Answer 5

Data Quality Improvement

Correct Response

2,3,4,5

Explanation

Please refer to page 462 of DMBOK2.

Knowledge Area

Data quality

Question 13

Some common data quality business rule types are:

Question Type

multi-select

Answer 1

Definitional conformance

Answer 2

Format compliance

Answer 3

Range conformance

Answer 4

Mapping conformance

Question 14

The Shewhart chart contains the following elements:

Question Type

multi-select

Answer 1

Plan

Answer 2

Utilization

Answer 3

Do

Answer 4

Check

Answer 5

Act

Answer 6

All of the above

Correct Response

1,3,4,5

Explanation

Please refer to page 463 of DMBOK2.

Knowledge Area

Data quality

Question 15

Issues caused by data entry processes include:

Question Type

multi-select

Answer 1

Training issues

Answer 2

List entry replacement

Answer 3

Software issues

Answer 4

Soft state issues

Answer 5

Change to business processes

Answer 6

Inconsistent business process execution

Correct Response

1,2,5,6

Explanation

Please refer to page 466-467 of DMBOK2.

Knowledge Area

Data quality

Question 16

Data quality issues only emerge at initial stages of the data lifecycle.

Question Type

multiple-choice

Answer 1

True

Answer 2

False

Correct Response

2

Explanation

Please refer to page 465 of DMBOK2.

Knowledge Area

Data quality

Question 17

Field overloading: Unnecessary data duplication is often a result of poor data management.

Question Type

multiple-choice

Answer 1

True

Answer 2

False

Correct Response

2

Explanation

Please refer to page 469 of DMBOK2.

Knowledge Area

Data quality

Question 18

Data profiling examples include:

Question Type

multi-select

Answer 1

Counts of null

Answer 2

Max/Min value

Answer 3

Max/Min length

Answer 4

Frequency distribution

Answer 5

Data type and format

Answer 6

None of the above

Correct Response

1,2,3,4,5

Explanation

Please refer to page 470 of DMBOK2.

Knowledge Area

Data quality

Question 19

Data profiling also includes cross-column analysis, which can identify overlapping or duplicate columns and expose embedded value dependencies.

Question Type

multiple-choice

Answer 1

True

Answer 2

False

Correct Response

1

Explanation

Please refer to page 470 of DMBOK2.

Knowledge Area

Data quality

Question 20

While the focus of data quality improvement efforts is often on the prevention of errors, data quality can also be improved through some forms of data processing.

Question Type

multiple-choice

Answer 1

True

Answer 2

False

Explanation

Please refer to page 470 of DMBOK2.

Knowledge Area

Data quality

Chapter 14

Question 1

Volume refers to the amount of data. Big Data often has thousands of entities or elements in billions of records.

Question Type

multiple-choice

Answer 1

True

Answer 2

False

Question 2

The list of V's include:

Question Type

multi-select

Answer 1

Volatility

Answer 2

Volume

Answer 3

Veracity

Answer 4

Viscosity

Answer 5

Variety

Answer 6

Validity

Correct Response

1,2,3,4,5

Explanation

Please refer to page 502 of DMBOK2.

Knowledge Area

Big data and data science

Question 3

Veracity refers to how difficult the data is to use or to integrate.

Question Type

multiple-choice

Answer 1

True

Answer 2

False

Correct Response

2

Explanation

Please refer to page 502 of DMBOK2.

Knowledge Area

Big data and data science

Question 4

Different storage volumes include:

Question Type

multi-select

Answer 1

Gigabyte

Answer 2

Petabyte

Answer 3

Perabyte

Answer 4

Exabyte

Answer 5

Tetrabyte

Answer 6

Terabyte

Correct Response

1,2,4,6

Explanation

Please refer to page 503 of DMBOK2.

Knowledge Area

Big data and data science

Question 5

Please select the answer that does not represent a machine learning algorithm:

Question Type

multiple-choice

Answer 1

Reinforcement learning

Answer 2

Supervised learning

Answer 3

Artificial learning

Answer 4

Unsupervised learning

Correct Response

3

Explanation

Please refer to page 506 of DMBOK2.

Knowledge Area

Big data and data science

Question 6

Machine learning explores the construction and study of learning algorithms.

Question Type

multiple-choice

Answer 1

True

Answer 2

False

Correct Response

1

Explanation

Please refer to page 506 of DMBOK2.

Knowledge Area

Big data and data science

Question 7

Please select the answer that best fits the following description: Contains only real-time data.

Question Type

multiple-choice

Answer 1

Batch layer

Answer 2

Speed layer

Answer 3

Serving layer

Answer 4

Real-time layer

Correct Response

2

Explanation

Please refer to page 505 of DMBOK2.

Knowledge Area

Big data and data science

Question 8

SBA is an abbreviation for service-based architecture.

Question Type

multiple-choice

Answer 1

True

Answer 2

False

Correct Response

1

Explanation

Please refer to page 505 of DMBOK2.

Knowledge Area

Big data and data science

Question 9

Data mining is a sub-field of supervised learning where users attempt to model data elements and predict future outcomes through the evaluation of probability estimates.

Question Type

multiple-choice

Answer 1

True

Answer 2

False

Correct Response

2

Explanation

Please refer to page 507 of DMBOK2.

Knowledge Area

Big data and data science

Question 10

Media monitoring and text analysis are automated methods for retrieving insights from large unstructured or semi-structured data, such as transaction data, social media, blogs, and web news sites.

Question Type

multiple-choice

Answer 1

True

Answer 2

False

Question 11

Data and text mining use a range of techniques, including:

Question Type

multi-select

Answer 1

Profiling

Answer 2

Application reduction

Answer 3

Association

Answer 4

Data reduction

Answer 5

Clustering

Answer 6

All of the above

Correct Response

1,3,4,5

Explanation

Please refer to page 508 of DMBOK2.

Knowledge Area

Big data and data science

Question 12

The first two steps in the data science process are:

Question Type

Multi-select

Answer 1

Define Big Data data strategy & Business Need(s)

Answer 2

Choose Data Sources

Answer 3

Develop Data Science Hypotheses and Mehods

Answer 4

Acquire & Ingest Data source(s)

1,2

Explanation

Please refer to page 501 of DMBOK2.

Knowledge Area

Big data and data science

Question 13

Input in the Big Data and data science context diagram include:

Question Type

multi-select

Answer 1

IT standards

Answer 2

Data sources

Answer 3

Business strategy & goals

Answer 4

Database standards

Question 14

Data science involves the iterative inclusion of data sources into models that develop insights. Dat science depends on:

Question Type

multi-select

Answer 1

Consistency

Answer 2

Rich data sources

Answer 3

Information alignment and analysis

Answer 4

Information delivery

Answer 5

Presentation of findings and data insights

Answer 6

All of the above

Correct Response

2,3,4,5

Explanation

Please refer to page 500 of DMBOK2.

Knowledge Area

Big data and data science

Question 15

The language used in file-based solutions is called MapReduce. This language has three main steps:

Question Type

multi-select

Answer 1

Map

Answer 2

Shuffle

Answer 3

Free

Answer 4

Terminate

Answer 5

Integrate

Answer 6

Reduce

Correct Response

1,2,6

Explanation

Please refer to page 519-520 of DMBOK2.

Knowledge Area

Big data and data science

Question 16

MPP is an abbreviation for Major Parallel Processing.

Question Type

multiple-choice

Answer 1

True

Answer 2

False

Question 17

Traditional tool sin data visualtization have both a data and a graphical component. Advanced visualization and discovery tools use in-memory architecture to allow users to interact with the data.

Question Type

multiple-choice

Answer 1

True

Answer 2

False

Correct Response

1

Explanation

Please refer to page 520 of DMBOK2.

Knowledge Area

Big data and data science

Question 18

Analytics models are associated with different depths of analysis, including:

Question Type

multi-select

Answer 1

Quality testing

Answer 2

Explanatory modeling

Answer 3

Descriptive modeling

Answer 4

Performance modeling

Answer 5

All of the above

Answer 6

None of the above

Question 19

Modeling Bid data is a non-technical challenge but critical if an organization that want to describe and govern its data.

Question Type

multiple-choice

Answer 1

True

Answer 2

False

Correct Response

2

Explanation

Please refer to page 522 of DMBOK2.

Knowledge Area

Big data and data science

Question 20

Business people must be fully engaged in order to realize benefits from the advanced analytics.

Question Type

multiple-choice

Answer 1

True

Answer 2

False

Correct Response

1

Explanation

Please refer to page 524 of DMBOK2.

Knowledge Area

Big data and data science

Chapter 15

Question 1

CMA is an abbreviation for Capability Maturity Assessment.

Question Type

multiple-choice

Answer 1

True

Answer 2

False

Correct Response

1

Explanation

Please refer to page 531 of DMBOK2.

Knowledge Area

Data Management Maturity Assessment

Question 2

Organizations conduct capability maturity assessments for a number of reasons, including:

Question Type

multi-select

Answer 1

Organizational change

Answer 2

Data management issues

Answer 3

Regulation

Answer 4

Data governance

Answer 5

Data modeling

Answer 6

New technology

Question 3

A Data Management Maturity Assessment (DMMA) can be used to evaluate data management overall, or it can be used to focus on a single Knowledge Area or even a single process.

Question Type

multiple-choice

Answer 1

True

Answer 2

False

Correct Response

1

Explanation

Please refer to page 532 of DMBOK2.

Knowledge Area

Data Management Maturity Assessment

Question 4

Deliverables in the data management maturity assessment context diagram include:

Question Type

multi-select

Answer 1

Maturity baseline

Answer 2

Roadmap

Answer 3

Executive briefings

Answer 4

Recommendations

Answer 5

Risk assessment

Answer 6

Ratings and ranks

Correct Response

1,2,3,4,5,6

Explanation

Please refer to page 533 of DMBOK2.

Knowledge Area

Data Management Maturity Assessment

Question 5

The primary goal of data management capability assessment is to evaluate the current state of critical data management activities in order to plan for improvement.

Question Type

multiple-choice

Answer 1

True

Answer 2

False

Correct Response

1

Explanation

Please refer to page 534 of DMBOK2.

Knowledge Area

Data Management Maturity Assessment

Question 6

When selecting a DMM framework one should consider of it is repeatable.

Question Type

multiple-choice

Answer 1

True

Answer 2

False

Correct Response

1

Explanation

Please refer to page 546 of DMBOK2.

Knowledge Area

Data Management Maturity Assessment

Question 7

The IBM Data Governance Council model is organized around four key categories. Select the answer that is not a category.

Question Type

multiple-choice

Answer 1

Outcomes

Answer 2

System Lifecycles

Answer 3

Enablers

Answer 4

Core disciplines

Answer 5

Supporting disciplines

Correct Response

2

Explanation

Please refer to page 538-539 of DMBOK2.

Knowledge Area

Data Management Maturity Assessment

Question 8

A communication plan includes an engagement model for stakeholders, the type of information to be shared, and the schedule for sharing information.

Question Type

multiple-choice

Answer 1

True

Answer 2

False

Correct Response

1

Explanation

Please refer to page 545 of DMBOK2.

Knowledge Area

Data Management Maturity Assessment

Question 9

Oversight for the DMMA process belongs to the Data Quality team.

Question Type

multiple-choice

Answer 1

True

Answer 2

False

Correct Response

2

Explanation

Please refer to page 548 of DMBOK2.

Knowledge Area

Data Management Maturity Assessment

Question 10

DMMA ratings represent a snapshot of the organization's capability level.

Question Type

multiple-choice

Answer 1

True

Answer 2

False

Correct Response

1

Explanation

Please refer to page 548 of DMBOK2.

Knowledge Area

Data Management Maturity Assessment

Chapter 16

Question 1

A critical step in data management organization design is identifying the best-fit operating model for the organization.

Question Type

multiple-choice

Answer 1

True

Answer 2

False

Correct Response

1

Explanation

Please refer to page 553 of DMBOK2.

Knowledge Area

Data Management Organization and Role Expectations

Question 2

RACI is an acronym that is made up of the following terms.

Question Type

multi-select

Answer 1

Control

Answer 2

Responsible

Answer 3

Accountable

Answer 4

Informed

Answer 5

Reliable

Answer 6

Consulted

Correct Response

2,3,4,6

Explanation

Please refer to page 554 of DMBOK2.

Knowledge Area

Data Management Organization and Role Expectations

Question 3

Decentralized informality can be made more formal through a documented series of connections and accountabilities via a RACI matrix.

Question Type

multiple-choice

Answer 1

True

Answer 2

False

Correct Response

1

Explanation

Please refer to page 554 of DMBOK2.

Knowledge Area

Data Management Organization and Role Expectations

Question 4

Data management organizational constructs include the following type of model.

Question Type

multi-select

Answer 1

Network operating model

Answer 2

Decentralized operating model

Answer 3

Centralized operating model

Answer 4

Federation operating model

Answer 5

Hybrid operating model

Answer 6

Integrated operating model

Correct Response

1,2,3,5

Explanation

Please refer to page 553-557 of DMBOK2.

Knowledge Area

Data Management Organization and Role Expectations

Question 5

Factors that have shown to play a key role in the success in the success of effective data management organizations does not include:

Question Type

multiple-choice

Answer 1

Clear vision

Answer 2

Orientation and training

Answer 3

Leadership alignment

Answer 4

IT sponsorship

Correct Response

4

Explanation

Please refer to page 559 of DMBOK2.

Knowledge Area

Data Management Organization and Role Expectations

Question 6

Communication should start later in the process as too many inputs will distort the vision.

Question Type

multiple-choice

Answer 1

True

Answer 2

False

Question 7

Disciplines within the enterprise architecture practice does not include:

Question Type

multiple-choice

Answer 1

Technology architecture

Answer 2

Application architecture

Answer 3

Information architecture

Answer 4

Service Architecture

Answer 5

Business architecture

Correct Response

4

Explanation

Please refer to page 566 of DMBOK2.

Knowledge Area

Data Management Organization and Role Expectations

Question 8

Data quality management is a key capability of a data management practice and organization.

Question Type

multiple-choice

Answer 1

True

Answer 2

False

Correct Response

1

Explanation

Please refer to page 566 of DMBOK2.

Knowledge Area

Data Management Organization and Role Expectations

Question 9

Data modeller: responsible for fata model version control an change control

Question Type

multiple-choice

Answer 1

True

Answer 2

False

Correct Response

2

Explanation

Please refer to page 569of DMBOK2.

Knowledge Area

Data Management Organization and Role Expectations

Question 10

Data architect: A senior analyst responsible for data architecture and data integration.

Question Type

multiple-choice

Answer 1

True

Answer 2

False

Correct Response

1

Explanation

Please refer to page 569 of DMBOK2.

Knowledge Area

Data Management Organization and Role Expectations

Chapter 17

Question 1

The neutral zone is one of the phases in the Bridges' transition phases.

Question Type

multiple-choice

Answer 1

True

Answer 2

False

Correct Response

1

Explanation

Please refer to page 575 of DMBOK2.

Knowledge Area

Data Management and Organizational Change Management

Question 2

Data management professionals who understand formal change management will be more successful in bringing about changes that will help their organizations get more value from their data. To do so, it is important to understand:

Question Type

multi-select

Answer 1

The triggers for effective change

Answer 2

Data architecture

Answer 3

How people experience changes

Answer 4

Data security

Answer 5

The barriers to change

Answer 6

Why change fails

Correct Response

1,3,5,6

Explanation

Please refer to page 573 of DMBOK2.

Knowledge Area

Data Management and Organizational Change Management

Question 3

Change only requires change agents in special circumstances, especially when there is little to no adoption.

Question Type

multiple-choice

Answer 1

True

Answer 2

False

2

Explanation

Please refer to page 574 of DMBOK2.

Knowledge Area

Data Management and Organizational Change Management

Question 4

Please select the transition phases in Bridges' Transition process:

Question Type

multi-select

Answer 1

The neutral zone

Answer 2

The new beginning

Answer 3

The ending

Answer 4

The transition

Answer 5

The translation

Answer 6

The game

Correct Response

1,2,3

Explanation

Please refer to page 575 of DMBOK2.

Knowledge Area

Data Management and Organizational Change Management

Question 5

As part of its transformation, the organization must identify and respond to different kinds of roadblocks. Please select the answer that is not a roadblock:

Question Type

multiple-choice

Answer 1

Active resistance

Answer 2

Psychological

Answer 3

Systematic

Answer 4

Structural

Correct Response

3

Explanation

Please refer to page 580 of DMBOK2.

Knowledge Area

Data Management and Organizational Change Management

Question 6

In an information management context, the short-term wins and goals often arise from the resolution of an identified problem.

Question Type

multiple-choice

Answer 1

True

Answer 2

False

Correct Response

1

Explanation

Please refer to page 580 of DMBOK2.

Knowledge Area

Data Management and Organizational Change Management

Question 7

The second stage of Kotter's eight stage process is:

Question Type

multiple-choice

Answer 1

Developing a vision and a strategy

Answer 2

Establishing a sense of urgency

Answer 3

Creating short term wins

Answer 4

Creating the guiding coalition

Correct Response

4

Explanation

Please refer to page 583 of DMBOK2.

Knowledge Area

Data Management and Organizational Change Management

Question 8

To push up the urgency level requires adding of the sources of complacency or increasing of their impact.

Question Type

multiple-choice

Answer 1

True

Answer 2

False

Correct Response

2

Explanation

Please refer to page 584 of DMBOK2.

Knowledge Area

Data Management and Organizational Change Management

Question 9

Bold means doing something that might cause short term pain, not just something that looks good in a marketing email.

Question Type

multiple-choice

Answer 1

True

Answer 2

False

Correct Response

1

Explanation

Please refer to page 585 of DMBOK2.

Knowledge Area

Data Management and Organizational Change Management

Question 10

An effective team is based on two simple foundations: trust and a common goal.

Question Type

multiple-choice

Answer 1

True

Answer 2

False

Correct Response

1

Explanation

Please refer to page 174 of DMBOK2.

Knowledge Area

Data Management and Organizational Change Management

Practice Test 1

Question 1

Please select the 2 frameworks that show high-level relationships that influence how an organization manages data.

Question Type

multi-select

Answer 1

DAMA DMBOK Hexagon

Answer 2

DAMA Wheel

Answer 3

Strategic Alignment Model

Answer 4

Amsterdam Information Model

Correct Response

3,4

Explanation

Please refer to page 33 of DMBOK2.

Knowledge Area

Data Management

Question 2

Please select the 3 visuals that depict DAMA's Data Management Framework.

Question Type

multi-select

Answer 1

The DAMA Wheel

Answer 2

The DAMA Octagon

Answer 3

The Environmental Factors hexagon

Answer 4

The Knowledge Area Context Diagram

Answer 5

The Data Quality Function Context Diagram

Correct Response

1,3,4

Explanation

Please refer to page 35 of DMBOK2.

Knowledge Area

Data Management

Question 3

Data Governance is at the centre if the data management activities, since governance is required for consistency within and balance between functions.

Question Type

multiple-choice

Answer 1

True

Answer 2

False

Correct Response

1

Explanation

Please refer to page 35 of DMBOK2.

Knowledge Area

Data Management

Question 4

Please select the correct component pieces that form part of an Ethical Handling Strategy and Roadmap.

Question Type

multi-select

Answer 1

Values Statement

Answer 2

Compliance framework

Answer 3

Roadmap

Answer 4

Emotions matrix

Answer 5

All of the above

Answer 6

None of the above

Question 5

Data professionals involved in Business Intelligence, analytics and Data Science are often responsible for data that describes: who people are; what people do; where people live; and how people are treated. The data can be misused and counteract the principles underlying data ethics.

Question Type

multiple-choice

Answer 1

True

Answer 2

False

Correct Response

1

Explanation

Please refer to page 63 of DMBOK2.

Knowledge Area

Data Handling Ethics

Question 6

Select the areas to consider when constructing an organization's operating model:

Question Type

multi-select

Answer 1

Value of the data to the organisation

Answer 2

Business model

Answer 3

Cultural Factors

Answer 4

Impact of the regulation

Answer 5

All of the above

Answer 6

None of the above

Correct Response

6

Explanation

Please refer to page 82 of DMBOK2.

Knowledge Area

Data Governance

Question 7

Development of goals, principles and policies derived from the data governance strategy will not guide the organization into the desired future state.

Question Type

multiple-choice

Answer 1

True

Answer 2

False

Correct Response

2

Explanation

Please refer to page 83 of DMBOK2.

Knowledge Area

Data Governance

Question 8

Layers of data governance are often part of the solution. This means determining where accountability should reside for stewardship activities and who the owners of the data are.

Question Type

multiple-choice

Answer 1

True

Answer 2

False

Correct Response

1

Explanation

Please refer to page 82 of DMBOK2.

Knowledge Area

Data Governance

Question 9

A change management program supporting formal data governance should focus communication on:

Question Type

multi-select

Answer 1

Promoting the value of data assets

Answer 2

Obtaining buy-in from all stakeholders

Answer 3

Implementing data management training

Answer 4

Monitoring the resistance

Answer 5

Implementing new metric and KPIs

Answer 6

Addressing all queries

Correct Response

1,3,5

Explanation

Please refer to page 85 of DMBOK2.

Knowledge Area

Data Governance

Question 10

Measuring the effects of change management on in five key areas including: Awareness of the need to change; Desire to participate and support the change; Knowledge about how to change; Ability to implement new skills and behaviors; and Reinforcement to keep the change in place.

Question Type

multiple-choice

Answer 1

True

Answer 2

False

Correct Response

1

Explanation

Please refer to page 85-86 of DMBOK2.

Knowledge Area

Data Governance

Question 11

Issue management is the process for identifying, quantifying, prioritizing and resolving data governance related issues, including:

Question Type

multi-select

Answer 1

Authority

Answer 2

Compliance

Answer 3

Conflicts

Answer 4

Contracts

Answer 5

Data Efficiency

Answer 6

All of the above

Correct Response

1,2,3,4

Explanation

Please refer to page 86 of DMBOK2.

Knowledge Area

Data Governance

Question 12

Data governance requires control mechanisms and procedures for, but not limited to, assignment and tracking of action items.

Question Type

multiple-choice

Answer 1

True

Answer 2

False

Question 13

Data governance requires control mechanisms and procedures for, but not limited to, identifying, capturing, logging and updating actions.

Question Type

multiple-choice

Answer 1

True

Answer 2

False

Correct Response

2

Explanation

Please refer to page 87 of DMBOK2.

Knowledge Area

Data Governance

Question 14

Examples of concepts that can be standardized within the data architecture knowledge area include:

Question Type

multi-select

Answer 1

Data security standards

Answer 2

Enterprise data models

Answer 3

Tool standards

Answer 4

System naming conventions

Answer 5

Data quality rules

Answer 6

None of the above

Correct Response

2,3,4

Explanation

Please refer to page 89 of DMBOK2.

Knowledge Area

Data Governance

Question 15

Sample value metrics for a data governance program include:

Question Type

multi-select

Answer 1

Achievements of goals and objectives

Answer 2

Effectiveness of communication

Answer 3

Effectiveness of education

Answer 4

Contributions to business objectives

Answer 5

Reduction of risk

Answer 6

Improved efficiency in operations

Correct Response

4,5,6

Explanation

Please refer to page 94 of DMBOK2.

Knowledge Area

Data Governance

Question 16

Wat data architecture designs represent should be clearly documented. Examples include:

Question Type

multi-select

Answer 1

Current

Answer 2

Preferred

Answer 3

Priority

Answer 4

Retirement

Answer 5

Emerging

Answer 6

All of the above

Correct Response

1,2,4,5

Explanation

Please refer to page 116 of DMBOK2.

Knowledge Area

Data Architecture

Question 17

When constructing models and diagrams during formalisation of data architecture there are certain characteristics that minimise distractions and maximize useful information. Characteristics include:

Question Type

multi-select

Answer 1

A clear and consistent legend

Answer 2

A match between all diagram objects and the legend

Answer 3

A clear and consistent line direction

Answer 4

A consistent line across display methods

Answer 5

Consistent object attributes

Answer 6

Linear symmetry

Correct Response

1,2,3,4,5,6

Explanation

Please refer to page 116-117 of DMBOK2.

Knowledge Area

Data Architecture

Question 18

Enterprise data architecture influences the scope boundaries of project and system releases. An example of influence is data replication control.

Question Type

multiple-choice

Answer 1

True

Answer 2

False

Question 19

Data flows map and document relationships between data and locations where global differences occur.

Question Type

multiple-choice

Answer 1

True

Answer 2

False

Correct Response

2

Explanation

Please refer to page 108 of DMBOK2.

Knowledge Area

Data Architecture

Question 20

Examples of business processes when constructing data flow diagrams include:

Question Type

multi-select

Answer 1

Order Management

Answer 2

Invoicing

Answer 3

Customer

Answer 4

Sales order

Answer 5

Marketing & Sales

Answer 6

Product Development

Question 21

Please select the option that correctly orders the models in decreasing level of detail:

Question Type

multiple-choice

Answer 1

Subject Area model, Conceptual model, Logical model, Logical & Physical models for a project.

Answer 2

Conceptual model, Subject Area model, Logical model, Logical & Physical models for a project.

Answer 3

Conceptual model, Logical model, Subject Area model, Logical & Physical models for a project.

Answer 4

Logical model, Conceptual model, Subject Area model, Logical & Physical models for a project.

Answer 5

None of the above

Explanation

Please refer to page 105-106 of DMBOK2.

Knowledge Area

Data Architecture

Question 22

The four main types of NoSQL databases are:

Question Type

multi-select

Answer 1

Document

Answer 2

Strategic

Answer 3

Key-value

Answer 4

Column-orientated

Answer 5

Row-orientated

Answer 6

Graph

Correct Response

1,3,4,6

Explanation

Please refer to page 143 of DMBOK2.

Knowledge Area

Data Modelling and Design

Question 23

SPARC published their three-schema approach to database management. The three key components were:

Question Type

multi-select

Answer 1

Conceptual

Answer 2

Logical

Answer 3

Internal

Answer 4

Generic

Answer 5

External

Question 24

Within projects, conceptual data modelling and logical data modelling are part of requirements planning and analysis activities, while physical data modelling is a design activity.

Question Type

multiple-choice

Answer 1

True

Answer 2

False

Correct Response

1

Explanation

Please refer to page 145 of DMBOK2.

Knowledge Area

Data Modelling and Design

Question 25

Please select the correct name for the PDM abbreviation when referring to modelling.

Question Type

multiple-choice

Answer 1

Physical Data Model

Answer 2

Physical Dimension Model

Answer 3

Photo Data Model

Answer 4

Probabilistic Dimension Model

Answer 5

Photo Dimensional Model

Answer 6

None of the above

Correct Response

1

Explanation

Please refer to page 148 of DMBOK2.

Knowledge Area

Data Modelling and Design

Question 26

A dimensional physical data model is usually a star schema, meaning there is one structure for each dimension.

Question Type

multiple-choice

Answer 1

True

Answer 2

False

Correct Response

1

Explanation

Please refer to page 148 of DMBOK2.

Knowledge Area

Data Modelling and Design

Question 27

There are several reasons to denormalize data. The first is to improve performance by:

Question Type

multi-select

Answer 1

Making tables more readable when no foreign key exists

Answer 2

Combining data from multiple other tables in advance to avoid costly run-time joins

Answer 3

Creating smaller copies of fata to reduce costly run-time calculations and/or table scans of large tables.

Answer 4

Pre-calculating and sorting costly data calculations to avoid runt-time system resource competition.

Answer 5

All of the above

Answer 6

None of the above

Correct Response

2,3,4

Explanation

Please refer to page 150 of DMBOK2.

Knowledge Area

Data Modelling and Design

Question 28

It is unwise to implement data quality checks to ensure that the copies of the attributes are correctly stored.

Question Type

multiple-choice

Answer 1

True

Answer 2

False

Correct Response

2

Explanation

Please refer to page 150 of DMBOK2.

Knowledge Area

Data Modelling and Design

Question 29

Normalisation is the process of applying rules in order to organise business complexity into stable data structures.

Question Type

multiple-choice

Answer 1

True

Answer 2

False

Correct Response

1

Explanation

Please refer to page 150 of DMBOK2.

Knowledge Area

Data Modelling and Design

Question 30

The deliverables of the data modelling process include:

Question Type

multi-select

Answer 1

Diagram

Answer 2

Definitions

Answer 3

Roadmap

Answer 4

Issues and outstanding questions

Answer 5

Lineage

Answer 6

Assessments

Question 31

To build models, data modellers heavily rely on previous analysis and modelling work.

Question Type

multiple-choice

Answer 1

True

Answer 2

False

Correct Response

1

Explanation

Please refer to page 153 of DMBOK2.

Knowledge Area

Data Modelling and Design

Question 32

Creating the CDM involves the following steps:

Question Type

multi-select

Answer 1

Select Scheme

Answer 2

Select Notation

Answer 3

Complete Initial CDM

Answer 4

Incorporate Enterprise Technology

Answer 5

Obtain Sign-off

Answer 6

All of the above

Correct Response

6

Explanation

Please refer to page 153-154 of DMBOK2.

Knowledge Area

Data Modelling and Design

Question 33

Quality Assurance Testing (QA) is used to test functionality against requirements.

Question Type

multiple-choice

Answer 1

True

Answer 2

False

Correct Response

1

Explanation

Please refer to page 183 of DMBOK2.

Knowledge Area

Data Storage and Operations

Question 34

Databases are categorized in three general ways:

Question Type

multi-select

Answer 1

Hierarchical

Answer 2

Non-relational

Answer 3

Warped

Answer 4

Accessible

Answer 5

Relational

Answer 6

None of the above

Correct Response

1,2,5

Explanation

Please refer to page 184 of DMBOK2.

Knowledge Area

Data Storage and Operations

Question 35

Hierarchical database model is the newest database model

Question Type

multiple-choice

Answer 1

True

Answer 2

False

Correct Response

2

Explanation

Please refer to page 184 of DMBOK2.

Knowledge Area

Data Storage and Operations

Question 36

Access to data for Multidimensional databases use a variant of SQL called MDX or Multidimensional eXpression.

Question Type

multiple-choice

Answer 1

True

Answer 2

False

Explanation

Please refer to page 185 of DMBOK2.

Knowledge Area

Data Storage and Operations

Question 37

Temporal aspects usually include:

Question Type

multi-select

Answer 1

Value time

Answer 2

Valid time

Answer 3

Transmitting time

Answer 4

Transaction time

Correct Response

2,4

Explanation

Please refer to page 185 of DMBOK2.

Knowledge Area

Data Storage and Operations

Question 38

In Resource Description Framework (RDF) terminology, a triple store is composed of a subject that denotes a resource, the predicate that expresses a relationship between the subject and the object, and the object itself.

Question Type

multiple-choice

Answer 1

True

Answer 2

False

Correct Response

1

Explanation

Please refer to page 188 of DMBOK2.

Knowledge Area

Data Storage and Operations

Question 39

Security Risks include elements that can compromise a network and/or database.

Question Type

multiple-choice

Answer 1

True

Answer 2

False

Correct Response

1

Explanation

Please refer to page 250 of DMBOK2.

Knowledge Area

Data Security

Question 40

When assessing security risks it is required to evaluate each system for the following:

Question Type

multi-select

Answer 1

The complexity of the data stored or in transit

Answer 2

The sensitivity of the data stored or in transit

Answer 3

The requirements to protect the data

Answer 4

The current security protections in place

Answer 5

All of the above

Answer 6

None of the above

Question 41

Controlling data availability requires management of user entitlements and of structures that technically control access based on entitlements.

Question Type

multiple-choice

Answer 1

True

Answer 2

False

Correct Response

1

Explanation

Please refer to page 253 of DMBOK2.

Knowledge Area

Data Security

Question 42

Lack of automated monitoring represents serious risks, including compliance risk.

Question Type

multiple-choice

Answer 1

True

Answer 2

False

Correct Response

2

Explanation

Please refer to page 254 of DMBOK2.

Knowledge Area

Data Security

Question 43

To mitigate risks, implement a network-based audit appliance, which can address most of the weaknesses associated with the native audit tools. This kind of appliance has the following benefits:

Question Type

multi-select

Answer 1

High performance

Answer 2

Separation of duties

Answer 3

Granular transaction tracking

Answer 4

Transaction time

Question 44

Data security internal audits ensure data security and regulatory compliance policies are followed should be conducted regularly and consistently.

Question Type

multiple-choice

Answer 1

True

Answer 2

False

Correct Response

1

Explanation

Please refer to page 255 of DMBOK2.

Knowledge Area

Data Security

Question 45

An organization will create an uncover valuable Metadata during the process of developing Data Integration and Interoperability solutions.

Question Type

multiple-choice

Answer 1

True

Answer 2

False

Correct Response

1

Explanation

Please refer to page 293 of DMBOK2.

Knowledge Area

Data Integration and Interoperability

Question 46

A Metadata repository contains information about the data in an organization, including:

Question Type

multi-select

Answer 1

Hierarchical

Answer 2

Data structure

Answer 3

Warped

Answer 4

Content

Answer 5

Business rules for managing data

Answer 6

None of the above

Correct Response

2,4,5

Explanation

Please refer to page 296 of DMBOK2.

Knowledge Area

Data Integration and Interoperability

Question 47

Data lineage is useful to the development of the data governance strategy.

Question Type

multiple-choice

Answer 1

True

Answer 2

False

Correct Response

2

Explanation

Please refer to page 298 of DMBOK2.

Knowledge Area

Data Integration and Interoperability

Question 48

Orchestration is the term used to describe how multiple processes are organized and executed in a system.

Question Type

multiple-choice

Answer 1

True

Answer 2

False

Correct Response

1

Explanation

Please refer to page 282 of DMBOK2.

Knowledge Area

Data Integration and Interoperability

Question 49

Possible application coupling designs include:

Question Type

multi-select

Answer 1

Value coupling

Answer 2

Relaxed coupling

Answer 3

Tight coupling

Answer 4

Loose coupling

Correct Response

3,4

Explanation

Please refer to page 282 of DMBOK2.

Knowledge Area

Data Integration and Interoperability

Question 50

Coupling describes the degree to which two systems are intertwined.

Question Type

multiple-choice

Answer 1

True

Answer 2

False

Correct Response

1

Explanation

Please refer to page 281 of DMBOK2.

Knowledge Area

Data Integration and Interoperability

Question 51

JSON is an open, lightweight standard format for data interchange.

Question Type

multiple-choice

Answer 1

True

Answer 2

False

Correct Response

1

Explanation

Please refer to page 334 of DMBOK2.

Knowledge Area

Document and content management

Question 52

Defining quality content requires understanding the context of its production and use, including:

Question Type

multi-select

Answer 1

Timing

Answer 2

Producers

Answer 3

Consumers

Answer 4

Delivery

Answer 5

Format

Answer 6

None of the above

Correct Response

1,2,3,4,5

Explanation

Please refer to page 342 of DMBOK2.

Knowledge Area

Document and content management

Question 53

One common KPI of e-discovery is cost reduction.

Question Type

multiple-choice

Answer 1

True

Answer 2

False

Correct Response

1

Explanation

Please refer to page 343 of DMBOK2.

Knowledge Area

Document and content management

Question 54

XML is the abbreviation for standard mark-up language.

Question Type

multiple-choice

Answer 1

True

Answer 2

False

Explanation

Please refer to page 334 of DMBOK2.

Knowledge Area

Document and content management

Question 55

ANSI 859 recommends taking into account the following criteria when determining which control level applies to a data asset:

Question Type

multi-select

Answer 1

Consequences of change to the enterprise or project

Answer 2

Project impact, if change will have significant cost or schedule consequences

Answer 3

Cost of providing and updating the asset

Answer 4

Need to reuse the asset or earlier versions of the assets

Correct Response

1,2,3,4

Explanation

Please refer to page 327 of DMBOK2.

Knowledge Area

Document and content management

Question 56

Resource Description Framework (RDF), a common framework used to describe information about any Web resource, is a standard model for data interchange in the Web.

Question Type

multiple-choice

Answer 1

True

Answer 2

False

Correct Response

1

Explanation

Please refer to page 335 of DMBOK2.

Knowledge Area

Document and content management

Question 57

Managing business party Master Data poses these unique challenges:

Question Type

multi-select

Answer 1

Difficulties in unique identification

Answer 2

Difficulties in unique dimensions

Answer 3

The number of data sources and the differences between them

Answer 4

Reference data anomaly detection

Correct Response

1,3,4

Explanation

Please refer to page 366 of DMBOK2.

Knowledge Area

Reference and master data

Question 58

Different types of product Master Data solutions include:

Question Type

multi-select

Answer 1

Product Data in Enterprise Resource Planning (ERP)

Answer 2

Product data in Manufacturing Execution Systems (MES)

Answer 3

Product Lifecycle Management (PLM)

Answer 4

People Lifecycle Product Management (PLPM)

Answer 5

None of the above

Question 59

Location Master Data includes business party addresses and business party location, as well as facility addresses for locations owned by organizations.

Question Type

multiple-choice

Answer 1

True

Answer 2

False

Correct Response

1

Explanation

Please refer to page 368 of DMBOK2.

Knowledge Area

Reference and master data

Question 60

There are three basic approaches to implementing a Master Data hub environment, including:

Question Type

multi-select

Answer 1

Transaction hub

Answer 2

Compliance hub

Answer 3

Consolidated hub

Answer 4

Emotions hub

Answer 5

Location hub

Answer 6

Registry

Correct Response

1,3,6

Explanation

Please refer to page 369-370 of DMBOK2.

Knowledge Area

Reference and master data

Question 61

All organizations have the same Master Data Management Drivers and obstacles.

Question Type

multiple-choice

Answer 1

True

Answer 2

False

Correct Response

2

Explanation

Please refer to page 371 of DMBOK2.

Knowledge Area

Reference and master data

Question 62

Type of Reference Data Changes include:

Question Type

multi-select

Answer 1

Creation of new Reference Data sets

Answer 2

Business model changes on column level

Answer 3

Row level changes to internal Reference Data sets

Answer 4

Row level changes to external Reference Data sets

Answer 5

Structural changes to external Reference Data sets

Answer 6

None of the above

Question 63

Sharing and using Reference and Master Data requires collaboration between multiple parties internal to the organization and sometimes with parties external to it.

Question Type

multiple-choice

Answer 1

True

Answer 2

False

Correct Response

2

Explanation

Please refer to page 377 of DMBOK2.

Knowledge Area

Reference and master data

Question 64

Those responsible for the data-sharing environment have an obligation to downstream data consumers to provide high quality data.

Question Type

multiple-choice

Answer 1

True

Answer 2

False

1

Explanation

Please refer to page 377 of DMBOK2.

Knowledge Area

Reference and master data

Question 65

Metrics tied to Reference and Master Data Quality include:

Question Type

multi-select

Answer 1

Service level agreements

Answer 2

Data sharing volume and usage

Answer 3

Implementing data management training

Answer 4

Data steward coverage

Answer 5

Data ingestion and consumption

Answer 6

Addressing all queries

Correct Response

1,2,4,5

Explanation

Please refer to page 379 of DMBOK2.

Knowledge Area

Reference and master data

Question 66

In the Data Warehousing and Business Intelligence Context Diagram, a primary deliverable is the DW and BI Architecture.

Question Type

multiple-choice

Answer 1

True

Answer 2

False

Correct Response

1

Explanation

Please refer to page 382 of DMBOK2.

Knowledge Area

Reference and master data

Question 67

The implementation of a Data Warehouse should follow guiding principles, including:

Question Type

multi-select

Answer 1

Collaborate

Answer 2

One size does not fit all

Answer 3

Focus on the business goals

Answer 4

Contracts

Answer 5

Data Efficiency

Answer 6

Start with the end in mind

Correct Response

1,2,3,6

Explanation

Please refer to page 383-384 of DMBOK2.

Knowledge Area

Data warehouse and business intelligence

Question 68

The Data Warehouse (DW) is a combination of three primary components: An integrated decision support database, related software programs and business intelligence reports.

Question Type

multiple-choice

Answer 1

True

Answer 2

False

Correct Response

2

Explanation

Please refer to page 384 of DMBOK2.

Knowledge Area

Data warehouse and business intelligence

Question 69

Data Warehouse describes the operational extract, cleansing, transformation, control and load processes that maintain the data in a data warehouse.

Question Type

multiple-choice

Answer 1

True

Answer 2

False

Correct Response

1

Explanation

Please refer to page 385 of DMBOK2.

Knowledge Area

Data warehouse and business intelligence

Question 70

Elements that point to differences between warehouses and operational systems include:

Question Type

multi-select

Answer 1

Data security standards

Answer 2

Integrated

Answer 3

Subject-orientated

Answer 4

Historical

Answer 5

Data quality

Answer 6

Non-volatile

Correct Response

2,3,4,5

Explanation

Please refer to page 386 of DMBOK2.

Knowledge Area

Data warehouse and business intelligence

Question 71

Corporate Information Factory (CIF) components include:

Question Type

multi-select

Answer 1

Objectives

Answer 2

Data marts

Answer 3

Staging Area

Answer 4

Contributions to business objectives

Answer 5

Reduction of risk

Answer 6

Operational Reports

Correct Response

2,3,6

Explanation

Please refer to page 386-387 of DMBOK2.

Knowledge Area

Data warehouse and business intelligence

Question 72

The DW encompasses all components in the data staging and data presentation areas, including:

Question Type

multi-select

Answer 1

Operational source system

Answer 2

Technology source system

Answer 3

Data staging area

Answer 4

Data presentation area

Answer 5

Data access tools

Answer 6

All of the above

Correct Response

1,3,4,5

Explanation

Please refer to page 389 of DMBOK2.

Knowledge Area

Data warehouse and business intelligence

Question 73

The warehouse has a set of storage areas, including:

Question Type

multi-select

Answer 1

Operational data store (ODS)

Answer 2

Data marts

Answer 3

Cubes

Answer 4

Staging area

Answer 5

Consistent object attributes

Answer 6

Central warehouse

Correct Response

1,2,3,4,6

Explanation

Please refer to page 391-392 of DMBOK2.

Knowledge Area

Data warehouse and business intelligence

Question 74

Data warehouses are often loaded and serviced by a nightly batch window.

Question Type

multiple-choice

Answer 1

True

Answer 2

False

Correct Response

1

Explanation

Please refer to page 393 of DMBOK2.

Knowledge Area

Data warehouse and business intelligence

Question 75

In gathering requirements for DW/BI projects, begin with the data goals and strategies first.

Question Type

multiple-choice

Answer 1

True

Answer 2

False

Correct Response

2

Explanation

Please refer to page 395 of DMBOK2.

Knowledge Area

Data warehouse and business intelligence

Question 76

Metadata management solutions include architectural layers including:

Question Type

multi-select

Answer 1

Metadata delivery

Answer 2

Metadata integration

Answer 3

Metadata usage

Answer 4

Metadata Sales

Answer 5

Metadata Marketing

Answer 6

Metadata control and management

Correct Response

1,2,3,6

Explanation

Please refer to page 431 of DMBOK2.

Knowledge Area

Metadata management

Question 77

An input in the Metadata management context diagram does not include:

Question Type

multiple-choice

Answer 1

Business requirements

Answer 2

Business metadata

Answer 3

Technical metadata

Answer 4

Metadata standards

Answer 5

Process Metadata

Correct Response

4

Explanation

Please refer to page 419 of DMBOK2.

Knowledge Area

Metadata management

Question 78

Poorly managed metadata leads to:

Question Type

multi-select

Answer 1

Document inefficiencies

Answer 2

Redundant data and data management processes

Answer 3

Doubt about the reliability of metadata and data

Answer 4

Redundant master data

Answer 5

Row-orientated metadata

Answer 6

Graph metadata issues

Correct Response

2,3

Explanation

Please refer to page 420 of DMBOK2.

Knowledge Area

Metadata management

Question 79

Metadata is described using three sets od categories, including:

Question Type

multi-select

Answer 1

Conceptual Metadata

Answer 2

Descriptive Metadata

Answer 3

Structural Metadata

Answer 4

Generic Metadata

Answer 5

Administrative metadata

Correct Response

2,3,5

Explanation

Please refer to page 422 of DMBOK2.

Knowledge Area

Metadata management

Question 80

Technical metadata describes details of the processing and accessing of data.

Question Type

multiple-choice

Answer 1

True

Answer 2

False

Correct Response

2

Explanation

Please refer to page 423 of DMBOK2.

Knowledge Area

Metadata management

Question 81

SOA stands for:

Question Type

multiple-choice

Answer 1

Service orientated architecture

Answer 2

Service orchestrated architecture

Answer 3

Service orientated access

Answer 4

Service overall architecture

Correct Response

1

Explanation

Please refer to page 430 of DMBOK2.

Knowledge Area

Metadata management

Question 82

An advantage of a centralized repository include: Quick metadata retrieval, since the repository and the query reside together.

Question Type

multiple-choice

Answer 1

True

Answer 2

False

Correct Response

1

Explanation

Please refer to page 431 of DMBOK2.

Knowledge Area

Metadata management

Question 83

Functionality-focused requirements associated with a comprehensive metadata solution, include:

Question Type

multi-select

Answer 1

Volatility

Answer 2

Synchronization

Answer 3

History

Answer 4

Access rights

Answer 5

Structure

Answer 6

None of the above

Correct Response

1,2,3,4,5

Explanation

Please refer to page 435-436 of DMBOK2.

Knowledge Area

Metadata management

Question 84

A general principle for managing metadata includes Responsibility.

Question Type

multiple-choice

Answer 1

True

Answer 2

False

Correct Response

2

Explanation

Please refer to page 438 of DMBOK2.

Knowledge Area

Metadata management

Question 85

A control activity in the metadata management environment includes loading statistical analysis.

Question Type

multiple-choice

Answer 1

True

Answer 2

False

Correct Response

1

Explanation

Please refer to page 437 of DMBOK2.

Knowledge Area

Metadata management

Question 86

Accomplish repository scanning in two distinct approaches, including:

Question Type

multi-select

Answer 1

Proprietary interface

Answer 2

Proprietary integration

Answer 3

Semi-proprietary interface

Answer 4

Semi- proprietary integration

Correct Response

1,3

Explanation

Please refer to page 439 of DMBOK2.

Knowledge Area

Metadata management

Question 87

Valuation information, as an example of data enrichment, is for asset valuation, inventory and sale.

Question Type

multiple-choice

Answer 1

True

Answer 2

False

Question 88

Examples of data enhancement includes:

Question Type

multi-select

Answer 1

Contextual information

Answer 2

Select Notation

Answer 3

Reference vocabularies

Answer 4

Incorporate Enterprise Technology

Answer 5

Audit data

Answer 6

All of the above

Correct Response

1,3,5

Explanation

Please refer to page 471-472 of DMBOK2.

Knowledge Area

Data quality

Question 89

Data parsing is the process of analysing data using pre-determined rules to define its content or value.

Question Type

multiple-choice

Answer 1

True

Answer 2

False

Correct Response

1

Explanation

Please refer to page 472 of DMBOK2.

Knowledge Area

Data quality

Question 90

Data quality rules and standards are a critical form of Metadata. Ti be effective they need to be managed as Metadata. Rules include:

Question Type

multi-select

Answer 1

Hierarchical consistency

Answer 2

Document consistency

Answer 3

Tied to business impact

Answer 4

Confirmed by SMEs

Answer 5

Accessible to all data customers

Answer 6

None of the above

Correct Response

2,3,4,5

Explanation

Please refer to page 478 of DMBOK2.

Knowledge Area

Data quality

Question 91

The most important reason to implement operational data quality measurements is to inform data consumers about levels of data effectiveness.

Question Type

multiple-choice

Answer 1

True

Answer 2

False

Question 92

Effective data management involves a set of complex, interrelated processes that disable an organization to use its data to achieve strategic goals.

Question Type

multiple-choice

Answer 1

True

Answer 2

False

Question 93

Inputs in the data quality context diagram include:

Question Type

multi-select

Answer 1

Data quality expectations

Answer 2

Business requirements

Answer 3

Data stores

Answer 4

Data lakes

Question 94

The term data quality refers to both the characteristics associated with high quality data and to the processes used to measure or improve the quality of data.

Question Type

multiple-choice

Answer 1

True

Answer 2

False

Correct Response

1

Explanation

Please refer to page 453 of DMBOK2.

Knowledge Area

Data quality

Question 95

Uniqueness, as a dimension of data quality, states no entity exists more than once within the data set.

Question Type

multiple-choice

Answer 1

True

Answer 2

False

Correct Response

1

Explanation

Please refer to page 459 of DMBOK2.

Knowledge Area

Data quality

Question 96

ISO 8000 will describe the structure and organization of data quality management, including:

Question Type

multi-select

Answer 1

Data Quality Audit

Answer 2

Data Quality Planning

 Answer 3

Data Quality Control

 Answer 4

Data Quality Assurance

 Answer 5

Data Quality Improvement

 Answer 6

None of the above

Correct Response

2,3,4,5

Explanation

Please refer to page 462 of DMBOK2.

Knowledge Area

Data quality

Question 97

Business rules describe why business should operate internally, in order to be successful and compliant with the outside world.

Question Type

multiple-choice

Answer 1

True

Answer 2

False

Correct Response

2

Explanation

Please refer to page 464 of DMBOK2.

Knowledge Area

Data quality

Question 98

Big data primarily refers specifically to the volume of the data.

Question Type

multiple-choice

Answer 1

True

Answer 2

False

Question 99

In the Abate Information Triangle the past moves through the following echelons befor it comes insight:

Question Type

multi-select

Answer 1

Data

Answer 2

Big data

Answer 3

Knowledge

Answer 4

Transactions

Answer 5

Information

Answer 6

Time

Correct Response

1,3,5

Explanation

Please refer to page 498 of DMBOK2.

Knowledge Area

Big data and data science

Question 100

The biggest business driver for developing organizational capabilities around Big Data and Data Science is the desire to find and act on business opportunities that may be discovered through data sets generated through a diversified range of processes.

Question Type

multiple-choice

Answer 1

True

Answer 2

False

Correct Response

1

Explanation

Please refer to page 498 of DMBOK2.

Knowledge Area

Big data and data science

Practice Test 2

Question 1

Activities that drive the goals in the context diagram are classified into the following phases:

Question Type

multiple-choice

Answer 1

Planning, Analysis, Design, Implementation & Maintenance

Answer 2

Plan, Do, Check, Act

Answer 3

Plan, Develop, Operate, Control

Answer 4

Measure, Develop, Implement, Monitor, Improve

Correct Response

3

Explanation

Please refer to page 37 of DMBOK2.

Knowledge Area

Data Management

Question 2

The DMBOK support's DAMA's mission by:

Question Type

multi-select

Answer 1

Providing a functional framework

Answer 2

Guides IT personnel to improve data management

Answer 3

Establish a common vocabulary

Answer 4

Serving as the fundamental reference guide

Correct Response

1,3,4

Explanation

Please refer to page 37 of DMBOK2.

Knowledge Area

Data Management

Question 3

Project that use personal data should have a disciplined approach to the use of that data. They should account for:

Question Type

multi-select

Answer 1

How they select their populations for study

Answer 2

How data will be captured

Answer 3

What activities analytics will focus on

Answer 4

How results will be made accessible

Answer 5

All of the above

Correct Response

5

Explanation

Please refer to page 63 of DMBOK2.

Knowledge Area

Data Handling Ethics

Question 4

Within each area of consideration mentioned in question 13, they should address morale adversity as per Ethical Risk Model for Sampling Projects.

Question Type

multiple-choice

Answer 1

True

Answer 2

False

Correct Response

2

Explanation

Please refer to page 63-64 of DMBOK2.

Knowledge Area

Data Handling Ethics

Question 5

DAMA International's Certified Data Management Professional (CDMP) certification required that data management professionals subscribe to a formal code of ethics, including an obligation to handle data ethically for the sake of society beyond the organization that employs them.

Question Type

multiple-choice

Answer 1

True

Answer 2

False

Correct Response

1

Explanation

Please refer to page 65 of DMBOK2.

Knowledge Area

Data Handling Ethics

Question 6

Business glossaries have the following objectives:

Question Type

multi-select

Answer 1

Enable common understanding of the core business concepts and terminology

Answer 2

Reduce the risk that data will be misused due to inconsistent understanding of the business concepts.

Answer 3

Cultural factors that might improve the concepts and terminology

Answer 4

Improve the alignment between technology assets and the business organization

Answer 5

Maximise search capability and enable access to documented institutional knowledge

Answer 6

All of the above

Correct Response

1,2,4,5

Explanation

Please refer to page 90 of DMBOK2.

Knowledge Area

Data Governance

Question 7

The target of organizational change is expedition.

Question Type

multiple-choice

Answer 1

True

Answer 2

False

Correct Response

2

Explanation

Please refer to page 94 of DMBOK2.

Knowledge Area

Data Governance

Question 8

Effectiveness metrics for a data governance programme includes: achievement of goals and objectives; extend stewards are using the relevant tools; effectiveness of communication; and effectiveness of education.

Question Type

multiple-choice

Answer 1

True

Answer 2

False

Question 9

Tools required to manage and communicate changes in data governance programs include

Question Type

multi-select

Answer 1

Business/Data Governance strategy map

Answer 2

Obtaining buy-in from all stakeholders

Answer 3

Data governance roadmap

Answer 4

Monitoring the resistance

Answer 5

Ongoing business case for data governance

Answer 6

Data governance metrics

Correct Response

1,3,5,6

Explanation

Please refer to page 94 of DMBOK2.

Knowledge Area

Data Governance

Question 10

When constructing an organization's operating model cultural factors must be taken into consideration.

Question Type

multiple-choice

Answer 1

True

Answer 2

False

1

Explanation

Please refer to page 81 of DMBOK2.

Knowledge Area

Data Governance

Question 11

Principles for data asset accounting include:

Question Type

multi-select

Answer 1

Due Diligence Principle

Answer 2

Going Concern Principle

Answer 3

Audit Principle

Answer 4

Asset Principle

Answer 5

Accounting Principle

Answer 6

All of the above

Correct Response

6

Explanation

Please refer to page 78 of DMBOK2.

Knowledge Area

Data Governance

Question 12

Data governance requires control mechanisms and procedures for, but not limited to, facilitating subjective discussions where managers' viewpoints are heard.

Question Type

multiple-choice

Answer 1

True

Answer 2

False

Correct Response

2

Explanation

Please refer to page 87 of DMBOK2.

Knowledge Area

Data Governance

Question 13

Data governance requires control mechanisms and procedures for, but not limited to, escalating issues to higher level of authority.

Question Type

multiple-choice

Answer 1

True

Answer 2

False

Correct Response

1

Explanation

Please refer to page 87 of DMBOK2.

Knowledge Area

Data Governance

Question 14

Examples of concepts that can be standardized within the data quality knowledge area include:

Question Type

multi-select

Answer 1

Data security standards

Answer 2

Data quality rules

Answer 3

Standard measurement methodologies

Answer 4

Data remediation standards and procedures

Answer 5

Data quality rules

Answer 6

None of the above

Correct Response

2,3,4

Explanation

Please refer to page 89 of DMBOK2.

Knowledge Area

Data Governance

Question 15

Several global regulations have significant implications on data management practices. Examples include:

Question Type

multi-select

Answer 1

Data Standards

Answer 2

SPCA

Answer 3

Effectiveness of education Standards

Answer 4

BCBS 239

Answer 5

PCI-DSS

Answer 6

Privacy laws

Correct Response

4,5,6

Explanation

Please refer to page 87 of DMBOK2.

Knowledge Area

Data Governance

Question 16

Please select the four domains of enterprise architecture:

Question Type

multi-select

Answer 1

Enterprise business architecture

Answer 2

Enterprise data architecture

Answer 3

Enterprise software architecture

Answer 4

Enterprise application architecture

Answer 5

Enterprise technology architecture

Answer 6

Enterprise hardware architecture

Correct Response

1,2,4,5

Explanation

Please refer to page 101-102 of DMBOK2.

Knowledge Area

Data Architecture

Question 17

Architects seek to design in a way that brings value to an organisation. To reach these goals, data architects define and maintain specifications that:

Question Type

multi-select

Answer 1

Align data architecture with enterprise strategy and business architecture

Answer 2

Define the current state of data in the organization.

Answer 3

Provide a standard business vocabulary for data and components

Answer 4

Express strategic data requirements

Answer 5

Integrate with overall enterprise architecture roadmap

Answer 6

Outline high-level integrated designs to meet these requirements.

Correct Response

1,2,3,4,5,6

Explanation

Please refer to page 101 of DMBOK2.

Knowledge Area

Data Architecture

Question 18

A deliverable in the data architecture context diagram includes an implementation roadmap.

Question Type

multiple-choice

Answer 1

True

Answer 2

False

Correct Response

1

Explanation

Please refer to page 100 of DMBOK2.

Knowledge Area

Data Architecture

Question 19

An input in the data architecture context diagram includes data governance.

Question Type

multiple-choice

Answer 1

True

Answer 2

False

Correct Response

2

Explanation

Please refer to page 100 of DMBOK2.

Knowledge Area

Data Architecture

Question 20

Enterprise data architecture description must include both [1] as well as [2]

Question Type

multiple-choice

Answer 1

[1] Enterprise Data Model [2] Data Context Diagram

Answer 2

[1] Enterprise Data Model [2] Architecture Diagram

Answer 3

[1] Data Flow Design [2] Data Context Diagram

Answer 4

[1] Enterprise Data Model [2] Data Flow Design

Correct Response

4

Explanation

Please refer to page 104 of DMBOK2.

Knowledge Area

Data Architecture

Question 21

Data and enterprise architecture deal with complexity from two viewpoints:

Question Type

multi-select

Answer 1

Innovation-orientated

Answer 2

Industry-orientated

Answer 3

Implementation-orientated

Answer 4

Quality-orientated

Answer 5

Architecture-orientated

Answer 6

None of the above

Correct Response

1,4

Explanation

Please refer to page 109-110 of DMBOK2.

Knowledge Area

Data Architecture

Question 22

Please select the correct name for the LDM abbreviation

Question Type

multiple-choice

Answer 1

Lifecycle Dimensional Model

Answer 2

Logical Dimensional Model

Answer 3

Lifecycle Data Model

Answer 4

Logical Data Model

Question 23

Logical abstraction entities become separate objects in the physical database design using one of two methods.

Question Type

multi-select

Answer 1

The DAMA Wheel

Answer 2

Subtype absorption

Answer 3

Subtype partition

Answer 4

Supertype absorption

Answer 5

Supertype partition

Correct Response

2,5

Explanation

Please refer to page 156 of DMBOK2.

Knowledge Area

Data Modelling and Design

Question 24

Data modelling tools are software that automate many of the tasks the data modeller performs.

Question Type

multiple-choice

Answer 1

True

Answer 2

False

Question 25

Small reference data value sets in the logical data model can be implemented in a physical model in three common ways:

Question Type

multi-select

Answer 1

Create a matching separate code table

Answer 2

Program integration by joining tables

Answer 3

Roadmap Development

Answer 4

Create a master shared code table

Answer 5

Embed rules or valid codes into the appropriate object's definition.

Answer 6

None of the above

Correct Response

1,4,5

Explanation

Please refer to page 157 of DMBOK2.

Knowledge Area

Data Modelling and Design

Question 26

The ISO 11179 Metadata registry, an international standard for representing Metadata in an organization, contains several sections related to data standards, including naming attributes and writing definitions.

Question Type

multiple-choice

Answer 1

True

Answer 2

False

Question 27

In designing and building the database, the DBA should keep the following design principles in mind:

Question Type

multi-select

Answer 1

Performance and ease of use

Answer 2

Reusability

Answer 3

Integrity

Answer 4

Security

Answer 5

Assessments

Answer 6

Maintainability

Correct Response

1,2,3,4,6

Explanation

Please refer to page 161-162 of DMBOK2.

Knowledge Area

Data Modelling and Design

Question 28

Data professional should not balance the short-term versus long-term business interests.

Question Type

multiple-choice

Answer 1

True

Answer 2

False

Correct Response

2

Explanation

Please refer to page 162 of DMBOK2.

Knowledge Area

Data Modelling and Design

Question 29

The Data Model Scorecard provides 10 data model quality metrics

Question Type

multiple-choice

Answer 1

True

Answer 2

False

Correct Response

2

Explanation

Please refer to page 164 of DMBOK2.

Knowledge Area

Data Modelling and Design

Question 30

The categories of the Data Model Scorecard with the highest weightings include:

Question Type

multi-select

Answer 1

How well does the model capture the requirements?

Answer 2

How complete is the model?

Answer 3

How good are the definitions?

Answer 4

How structurally sound is the model?

Answer 5

All of the above

Answer 6

None of the above

Question 31

Subtype absorption: The subtype entity attributes are included as nullable columns into a table representing the supertype entity

Question Type

multiple-choice

Answer 1

True

Answer 2

False

Question 32

Please select the three types of data models:

Question Type

multi-select

Answer 1

Dimensional Data model

Answer 2

Physical Data Model

Answer 3

Idea Data Model

Answer 4

Logical Data Model

Answer 5

Conceptual Data Model

Answer 6

Innovative Data Model

Question 33

Archiving is the process of moving data off immediately accessible storage media and onto media with lower retrieval performance.

Question Type

multiple-choice

Answer 1

True

Answer 2

False

Correct Response

1

Explanation

Please refer to page 189 of DMBOK2.

Knowledge Area

Data Storage and Operations

Question 34

Triplestores can be classified into these categories:

Question Type

multi-select

Answer 1

Native triplestores

Answer 2

MapReduce triplestores

Answer 3

RDMS-backed triplestores

Answer 4

NoSQL triplestores

Answer 5

All of the above

Answer 6

None of the above

2,3,4

Explanation

Please refer to page 188 of DMBOK2.

Knowledge Area

Data Storage and Operations

Question 35

Data replication can be active or passive.

Question Type

multiple-choice

Answer 1

True

Answer 2

False

Correct Response

1

Explanation

Please refer to page 191 of DMBOK2.

Knowledge Area

Data Storage and Operations

Question 36

Data replication has two dimensions of scaling: diagonal and lateral

Question Type

multiple-choice

Answer 1

True

Answer 2

False

Correct Response

2

Explanation

Please refer to page 191 of DMBOK2.

Knowledge Area

Data Storage and Operations

Question 37

There are three recovery types that provide guidelines for how quickly recovery takes place and what it focuses on.

Question Type

multi-select

Answer 1

Immediate recovery

Answer 2

Critical recovery

Answer 3

Non-critical recovery

Answer 4

Intermittent recovery

Answer 5

Translucent recovery

Answer 6

BMT recovery

Correct Response

1,2,3

Explanation

Please refer to page 192-193 of DMBOK2.

Knowledge Area

Data Storage and Operations

Question 38

DBAs and database architects combine their knowledge of available tools with the business requirements in order to suggest the best possible application of technology to meet organizational goals.

Question Type

multiple-choice

Answer 1

True

Answer 2

False

Question 39

A hacker is a person who finds unknown operations and pathways within complex computer system. Hackers are only bad.

Question Type

multiple-choice

Answer 1

True

Answer 2

False

Correct Response

2

Explanation

Please refer to page 241 of DMBOK2.

Knowledge Area

Data Security

Question 40

Device security standard include:

Question Type

multi-select

Answer 1

Access policies regarding connections using mobile devices

Answer 2

Installation of anti-malware and encryption software

Answer 3

Regulation compliance standards

Answer 4

Awareness of security vulnerabilities

Answer 5

Relational security policies

Answer 6

None of the above

Question 41

Service accounts are convenient because they can tailor enhanced access for the processes that use them.

Question Type

multiple-choice

Answer 1

True

Answer 2

False

Correct Response

1

Explanation

Please refer to page 240 of DMBOK2.

Knowledge Area

Data Security

Question 42

In a SQL injection attack, a perpetrator inserts authorized database statements into a vulnerable SQL data channel, such as a stored procedure.

Question Type

multiple-choice

Answer 1

True

Answer 2

False

Correct Response

2

Explanation

Please refer to page 241 of DMBOK2.

Knowledge Area

Data Security

Question 43

Lack of automated monitoring represents serious risks, including:

Question Type

multi-select

Answer 1

Risk of reliance on inadequate native

Answer 2

Risk of compliance

Answer 3

Direction and recovery risk

Answer 4

Administrative and audit duties risk

Correct Response

1,3,4

Explanation

Please refer to page 254 of DMBOK2.

Knowledge Area

Data Security

Question 44

A metadata repository is essential to assure the integrity and consistent use of an enterprise data model across business processes.

Question Type

Multiple-choice

Answer 1

True

Answer 2

False

Correct Response

1

Explanation

Please refer to page 258 of DMBOK2.

Knowledge Area

Data Security

Question 45

Enterprise service buses (ESB) are the data integration solution for near real-time sharing of data between many systems, where the hub is a virtual concept of the standard format or the canonical model for sharing data in the organization.

Question Type

multiple-choice

Answer 1

True

Answer 2

False

Correct Response

1

Explanation

Please refer to page 281 of DMBOK2.

Knowledge Area

Data Integration and Interoperability

Question 46

Examples of transformation in the ETL process onclude:

Question Type

multi-select

Answer 1

Hierarchical changes

Answer 2

Structure changes

Answer 3

De-duping

Answer 4

Re-ordering

Answer 5

Semantic conversions

Answer 6

None of the above

Correct Response

2,3,4,5

Explanation

Please refer to page 273-274 of DMBOK2.

Knowledge Area

Data Integration and Interoperability

Question 47

The load step of the ETL is physically storing or presenting the results of the transformation into the source system.

Question Type

multiple-choice

Answer 1

True

Answer 2

False

Correct Response

2

Explanation

Please refer to page 274 of DMBOK2.

Knowledge Area

Data Integration and Interoperability

Question 48

If the target system has more transformation capability than either the source or the intermediary application system, the order of processes may be switched to ELT – Extract Load Tranform.

Question Type

multiple-choice

Answer 1

True

Answer 2

False

Correct Response

1

Explanation

Please refer to page 274 of DMBOK2.

Knowledge Area

Data Integration and Interoperability

Question 49

Inputs in the Data Integration and Interoperability context diagram include:

Question Type

multi-select

Answer 1

Data semantics

Answer 2

Source data

Answer 3

Business goals & strategies

Answer 4

Data needs & standards

Question 50

The definition for Data Integration and Interoperability include Managing the movement and consolidation of data within and between applications and organizations.

Question Type

multiple-choice

Answer 1

True

Answer 2

False

Question 51

XML provides a language for representing both structures and unstructured data and information.

Question Type

multiple-choice

Answer 1

True

Answer 2

False

Correct Response

1

Explanation

Please refer to page 334 of DMBOK2.

Knowledge Area

Document and content management

Question 52

The information governance maturity model describes the characteristics of the information governance and recordkeeping environment at five levels of maturity for each of the eight GARP principles. Please select the correct level descriptions:

Question Type

multi-select

Answer 1

Level 2 In Development

Answer 2

Level 3 Essential

Answer 3

Level 4 Proactive

Answer 4

Level 3 Transformational

Answer 5

Level 2 Sub-standard

Answer 6

Level 4 Proactive

Question 53

A e-discovery readiness assessment should examine and identify opportunities for the commercial response program.

Question Type

multiple-choice

Answer 1

True

Answer 2

False

Correct Response

2

Explanation

Please refer to page 339 of DMBOK2.

Knowledge Area

Document and content management

Question 54

One of the percentages to measure success of a records management system implantation is the percentage of the identified corporate records declared as such and put under records control.

Question Type

multiple-choice

Answer 1

True

Answer 2

False

Correct Response

1

Explanation

Please refer to page 343 of DMBOK2.

Knowledge Area

Document and content management

Question 55

Some document management systems have a module that may support different types of workflows, such as:

Question Type

multi-select

Answer 1

Dynamic rules that allow for different workflows based in content

Answer 2

Rules that workflow as the data requirements change

Answer 3

Manual workflows that indicate where the user send the document

Answer 4

Transaction time to audit and log data flow

Correct Response

1,3

Explanation

Please refer to page 331 of DMBOK2.

Knowledge Area

Document and content management

Question 56

Effective document management requires clear policies and procedures, especially regarding retention and disposal of records.

Question Type

multiple-choice

Answer 1

True

Answer 2

False

Explanation

Please refer to page 328 of DMBOK2.

Knowledge Area

Document and content management

Question 57

Metrics tied to Reference and Master Data quality include:

Question Type

multi-select

Answer 1

Total cost of ownership

Answer 2

Data change activity

Answer 3

Strategic usage reporting

Answer 4

Amsterdam Information Model

Correct Response

1,2

Explanation

Please refer to page 379 of DMBOK2.

Knowledge Area

Reference and master data

Question 58

The first two steps of the Reference data Change request process, as prescribed DMBOk2, include:

Question Type

multi-select

Answer 1

Decide and Communicate

Answer 2

Update and Inform

Answer 3

Identify Stakeholder

Answer 4

Receive Change Request

Answer 5

Identify Impact

Question 59

Those responsible for the data-sharing environment have an obligation to downstream data consumers to provide high quality data.

Question Type

multiple-choice

Answer 1

True

Answer 2

False

Correct Response

1

Explanation

Please refer to page 377 of DMBOK2.

Knowledge Area

Reference and master data

Question 60

Reference and master data require governance processes, including:

Question Type

multi-select

Answer 1

 The data sources to be integrated

Answer 2

Compliance framework

Answer 3

The conditions of use rules to be followed

Answer 4

Emotions matrix

Answer 5

The priority and response levels of data stewardship efforts

Answer 6

None of the above

1,3,5

Explanation

Please refer to page 378 of DMBOK2.

Knowledge Area

Reference and master data

Question 61

Changes to reference data do not need to be management, only metadata should be managed.

Question Type

multiple-choice

Answer 1

True

Answer 2

False

Correct Response

2

Explanation

Please refer to page 376 of DMBOK2.

Knowledge Area

Reference and master data

Question 62

Inputs in the reference and master data context diagram include:

Question Type

multi-select

Answer 1

Business Drivers

Answer 2

Business model

Answer 3

Cultural Drivers

Answer 4

Data Glossary

Answer 5

All of the above

Answer 6

None of the above

Question 63

A business driver for Master Data Management program is managing data quality.

Question Type

multiple-choice

Answer 1

True

Answer 2

False

Correct Response

1

Explanation

Please refer to page 349 of DMBOK2.

Knowledge Area

Reference and master data

Question 64

A goal of a Reference and Master Data Management program include enabling master and reference data to be shared across enterprise functions and applications.

Question Type

multiple-choice

Answer 1

True

Answer 2

False

Question 65

Reference and Master Data Management follow these guiding principles:

Question Type

multi-select

Answer 1

Controlled change

Answer 2

Obtaining buy-in from all stakeholders

Answer 3

Ownership

Answer 4

Monitoring the resistance

Answer 5

Stewardship

Answer 6

Addressing all queries

Question 66

An implemented warehouse and its customer-facing BI tools is a technology product.

Question Type

multiple-choice

Answer 1

True

Answer 2

False

Correct Response

2

Explanation

Please refer to page 399 of DMBOK2.

Knowledge Area

Reference and master data

Question 67

The impact of the changes from new volatile data must be isolated from the bulk of the historical, non-volatile DW data. There are three main approaches, including:

Question Type

multi-select

Answer 1

Trickle Feeds

Answer 2

Data

Answer 3

Messaging

Answer 4

Technology

Answer 5

Streaming

Answer 6

All of the above

Question 68

The best DW/BI architects will design a mechanism to connect back to transactional level and operational level reports in an atomic DW.

Question Type

multiple-choice

Answer 1

True

Answer 2

False

Question 69

Implementing a BI portfolio is about identifying the right tools for the right user communities within or across business units.

Question Type

multiple-choice

Answer 1

True

Answer 2

False

Correct Response

1

Explanation

Please refer to page 398 of DMBOK2.

Knowledge Area

Data warehouse and business intelligence

Question 70

Typically, DW/BI projects have three concurrent development tracks, including:

Question Type

multi-select

Answer 1

Trickle Feeds

Answer 2

Data

Answer 3

Messaging

Answer 4

Technology

Answer 5

Streaming

Answer 6

BI Tools

2,4,6

Explanation

Please refer to page 396 of DMBOK2.

Knowledge Area

Data warehouse and business intelligence

Question 71

BI tool types include:

Question Type

multi-select

Answer 1

Operational reporting

Answer 2

Diagnostic, self-service analytics

Answer 3

Data lake extraction

Answer 4

BPM

Answer 5

Reduction of risk

Answer 6

Descriptive, self-service analytics

Correct Response

1,4,6

Explanation

Please refer to page 404 of DMBOK2.

Knowledge Area

Data warehouse and business intelligence

Question 72

Common OLAP operations include:

Question Type

multi-select

Answer 1

Cut

Answer 2

Slice

Answer 3

Dice

Answer 4

Roll-up

Answer 5

Drill down/up

Answer 6

All of the above

Correct Response

2,3,4,5

Explanation

Please refer to page 407 of DMBOK2.

Knowledge Area

Data warehouse and business intelligence

Question 73

Critical success factors throughout the BI/DW lifecycle include:

Question Type

multi-select

Answer 1

A clear and consistent focus

Answer 2

Business sponsorship

Answer 3

Business readiness

Answer 4

A consistent line across display methods

Answer 5

Vision alignment

Answer 6

Linear symmetry

Correct Response

2,4,5

Explanation

Please refer to page 410 of DMBOK2.

Knowledge Area

Data warehouse and business intelligence

Question 74

Business Intelligence, among other things, refer to the technology that supports this kind of analysis.

Question Type

multiple-choice

Answer 1

True

Answer 2

False

Correct Response

1

Explanation

Please refer to page 384 of DMBOK2.

Knowledge Area

Data warehouse and business intelligence

Question 75

The data warehouse and marts differ from that in applications as the data is organized by subject rather than function.

Question Type

multiple-choice

Answer 1

True

Answer 2

False

Correct Response

1

Explanation

Please refer to page 387 of DMBOK2.

Knowledge Area

Data warehouse and business intelligence

Question 76

Deliverables in the Metadata Management context diagram include:

Question Type

multi-select

Answer 1

Metadata Strategy

Answer 2

Metadata Standards

Answer 3

Data Lineage

Answer 4

Metadata Architecture

Answer 5

Metadata design

Answer 6

Data storage and operations

Correct Response

1,2,3,4

Explanation

Please refer to page 419 of DMBOK2.

Knowledge Area

Metadata management

Question 77

Metadata is described using different set of categories, including:

Question Type

multiple-choice

Answer 1

Prescriptive Metadata, Serial Metada, Administrative Metadata

Answer 2

Diagnostic Metadata, Structural Metada, Administrative Metadata

Answer 3

Descriptive Metadata, Serial Metada, Administrative Metadata

Answer 4

Descriptive Metadata, Structural Metada, Administrative Metadata

Answer 5

None of the above

Correct Response

4

Explanation

Please refer to page 422 of DMBOK2.

Knowledge Area

Metadata management

Question 78

Types of metadata include:

Question Type

multi-select

Answer 1

Technical

Answer 2

Strategic

Answer 3

Operational

Answer 4

Column-orientated

Answer 5

Business

Answer 6

Graph

Correct Response

1,3,5

Explanation

Please refer to page 423 of DMBOK2.

Knowledge Area

Metadata management

Question 79

Examples of technical metadata include:

Question Type

multi-select

Answer 1

Conceptual

Answer 2

Access permissions

Answer 3

Internal

Answer 4

ETL job details

Answer 5

Column Properties

Question 80

Structural Metadata describe srealtionships within and among resource and enables identification and retrieval.

Question Type

multiple-choice

Answer 1

True

Answer 2

False

Question 81

Please select the user that best describes the following description: Uses the business glossary to make architecture, systems design, and development decisions, and to conduct the impact analysis.

Question Type

multiple-choice

Answer 1

Business user

Answer 2

Analytical user

Answer 3

Technical user

Answer 4

Advanced user

Answer 5

None of the above

Correct Response

3

Explanation

Please refer to page 427 of DMBOK2.

Knowledge Area

Metadata management

Question 82

SOA is an abbreviation for service orientated architecture.

Question Type

multiple-choice

Answer 1

True

Answer 2

False

Correct Response

1

Explanation

Please refer to page 430 of DMBOK2.

Knowledge Area

Metadata management

Question 83

Advantages if a centralized metadata repository include:

Question Type

multi-select

Answer 1

Low latency, since it is independent of the source systems

Answer 2

Combining data from multiple other tables in advance to avoid costly run-time joins

Answer 3

Quick metadata retrieval

Answer 4

High availability

Answer 5

All of the above

Answer 6

None of the above

Correct Response

3,4

Explanation

Please refer to page 431 of DMBOK2.

Knowledge Area

Metadata management

Question 84

A limitation of the centralized metadata repository approach is it may be less expensive.

Question Type

multiple-choice

Answer 1

True

Answer 2

False

Correct Response

2

Explanation

Please refer to page 431 of DMBOK2.

Knowledge Area

Metadata management

Question 85

A completely distributed architecture maintains a single access point. The metadata retrieval engine responds to user requests by retrieving data from source systems in real time.

Question Type

multiple-choice

Answer 1

True

Answer 2

False

1

Explanation

Please refer to page 432 of DMBOK2.

Knowledge Area

Metadata management

Question 86

Control activities to manage metadata stores include:

Question Type

multi-select

Answer 1

Load statistical analysis

Answer 2

Definitions resolutions improvement

Answer 3

Roadmap extrapolation

Answer 4

Missing metadata reports

Answer 5

Lineage

Answer 6

Job scheduling and monitoring

Question 87

Many people assume that most data quality issues are caused by data entry errors. A more sophisticated understanding recognizes that gaps in or execution of business and technical processes cause many more problems that mis-keying.

Question Type

multiple-choice

Answer 1

True

Answer 2

False

Correct Response

1

Explanation

Please refer to page 465 of DMBOK2.

Knowledge Area

Data quality

Question 88

Issues caused by data entry processes include:

Question Type

multi-select

Answer 1

Field overloading

Answer 2

Data entry interface issues

Answer 3

Training issues

Answer 4

List entry placement

Answer 5

Changes to business processes

Answer 6

None of the above

Correct Response

1,2,3,4,5

Explanation

Please refer to page 466-467 of DMBOK2.

Knowledge Area

Data quality

Question 89

Data quality issues cannot emerge at any point in the data lifecycle.

Question Type

multiple-choice

Answer 1

True

Answer 2

False

Question 90

Barriers to effective management of data quality include:

Question Type

multi-select

Answer 1

Lack of awareness on the part of leadership and staff

Answer 2

Lack of business governance

Answer 3

Lack of leadership and management

Answer 4

Difficulty in justification of improvements

Answer 5

Inappropriate or ineffective instruments to measure value

Answer 6

None of the above

Correct Response

1,2,3,4,5

Explanation

Please refer to page 466 of DMBOK2.

Knowledge Area

Data quality

Question 91

Data profiling is a form of data analysis used to inspect data and assess quality.

Question Type

multiple-choice

Answer 1

True

Answer 2

False

Question 92

Improving data quality requires a strategy that accounts for the work that needs to be done and the way people will execute it.

Question Type

multiple-choice

Answer 1

True

Answer 2

False

Correct Response

1

Explanation

Please refer to page 474 of DMBOK2.

Knowledge Area

Data quality

Question 93

All data is of equal importance. Data quality management efforts should be spread between all the data in the organization.

Question Type

multiple-choice

Answer 1

True

Answer 2

False

Question 94

Once the most critical business needs and the data that supports them have been identified, the most important part of the data quality assessment is actually looking data, querying it to understand data content and relationships, and comparing actual data to rules and expectations.

Question Type

multiple-choice

Answer 1

True

Answer 2

False

Question 95

The operational data quality management procedures depend on the ability to measure and monitor the applicability of data.

Question Type

multiple-choice

Answer 1

True

Answer 2

False

Question 96

The best preventative action to prevent poor quality data from entering an organisation include:

Question Type

multi-select

Answer 1

Institute a formal change control

Answer 2

Define and enforce rules

Answer 3

Train data procedures

Answer 4

Implement data governance and stewardship

Answer 5

Establish data entry controls

Answer 6

None of the above

Correct Response

1,2,3,4,5

Explanation

Please refer to page 486 of DMBOK2.

Knowledge Area

Data quality

Question 97

Corrective actions are implemented after a problem has occurred and been detected.

Question Type

multiple-choice

Answer 1

True

Answer 2

False

Correct Response

1

Explanation

Please refer to page 486 of DMBOK2.

Knowledge Area

Data quality

Question 98

Data science merges data mining, statistical analysis, and machine learning with the integration and data modelling capabilities, to build predictive models that explore data content patterns.

Question Type

multiple-choice

Answer 1

True

Answer 2

False

Correct Response

1

Explanation

Please refer to page 500 of DMBOK2.

Knowledge Area

Big data and data science

Question 99

Data science depends on:

Question Type

multi-select

Answer 1

Rich data sources

Answer 2

Information alignment and analysis

Answer 3

Information delivery

Answer 4

Presentation of findings and data insights

Correct Response

1,2,3,4

Explanation

Please refer to page 500 of DMBOK2.

Knowledge Area

Big data and data science

Question 100

In the context of big data the Three V's refer to: Volume, Velocity and Validity

Question Type

multiple-choice

Answer 1

True

Answer 2

False

Correct Response

2

Explanation

Please refer to page 502 of DMBOK2.

Knowledge Area

Big data and data science

Printed in Great Britain
by Amazon

86116276R00281